The African American Struggle for Library Equality

The African American Struggle for Library Equality

The Untold Story of the Julius Rosenwald Fund Library Program

Aisha M. Johnson-Jones

ROWMAN & LITTLEFIELD
Lanham • Boulder • New York • London

Published by Rowman & Littlefield
An imprint of The Rowman & Littlefield Publishing Group, Inc.
4501 Forbes Boulevard, Suite 200, Lanham, Maryland 20706
www.rowman.com

6 Tinworth Street, London SE11 5AL

British Library Cataloguing in Publication Information Available

Library of Congress Cataloging-in-Publication Data Available

ISBN 978-1-5381-0308-1 (hbk)
ISBN 978-1-5381-0309-8 (electronic)

To Julius Rosenwald, an unsung hero and friend
to a culture at a disadvantage by design.

To every lover of archives, museums, and libraries.
This is for you. Never pick a side.

Contents

Preface

I wrote this book to acknowledge and bring awareness to the varying contributions of a mere man who desired to improve the lives of African Americans through increased educational opportunities. This is for every person who has casually walked into a library without thought of restrictions to access or services, for those who have freely browsed the open stacks not looking for a room guarded by a "Colored Only" sign, and for each patron who has checked out a book and simply walked out the front door.

Libraries were one of the many institutions used to oppress black culture, yet all facets of library history as it relates to early 20th-century access for African Americans, and philanthropic efforts to resolve the lack thereof, are understudied. Other forms of library and information science (LIS) research are more dedicated to identifying laws of human conduct (information behavior) and analyzing information retrieval systems, unintentionally forging a gap in LIS scholarship in its cross-pollination with other fields, including education, history, and public administration. Thus the purpose of the book also includes what I can offer to scholarship across disciplines by covering a range of subjects in American history, with a focus on African American literacy, black librarianship, black college libraries, public library history, and library philanthropy. Such research can uncover the unknown, answer questions, identify relationships between the past and present through archival records, and evaluate the basis of social movements. Historical research can also allow for garnering new insights concerning social processes external to the library because such customs or exercises often affect internal library practices. A perfect example is the de jure and de facto segregation in the 20th-century South, which unlawfully extended to all public accommodations, including education.

The refusal to grant one an education is based on the ability to read, write, and access free education. This act, among others based in violence, was committed against an entire culture, reinforcing white supremacy, and began with slavery—although house slaves were often taught to read in order to benefit their owners and carry out daily tasks. Slaves were also read to from the Bible. However, this access was manipulative, as slaves were provided a Bible in which passages of liberation and freedom had been removed. Naturally, secret meetings began to occur and reading lessons would take place. Slaves stole away in the night to a variety of locations, including meetings areas, fields where they labored over tightly packed crops, and shallow shacks. As the cold wind whistled, they taught each other to read and write. But slavery and education were incompatible. Slavery was suitable for the social norms of an inferior culture where people were treated as property and landowners depended on free labor, and it was crucial to continue to breed African American illiteracy.

Library history provides a biographical narrative concerning a geographic region, a library type, or a single library system as case study. This account often includes information on the establishment of the library, special benefactors, significant collections, services rendered, outstanding achievements, and other points of interest for the investigator. Southern states arguably possess the richest library history due to the region's delayed development accompanied by historical racism. This is one of the reasons philanthropists are drawn to the region. In addition, the art of storytelling gives the reader repeated opportunities to become engulfed by subjects, including the foundation of the American public library, access and services in the early 20th century, systematic delayed access to African Americans, the Julius Rosenwald Fund Library Program, and the survival of libraries in historically black colleges and universities (HBCUs). Historical research examines past events or a combination of occurrences in order to arrive at an explanation of a specific phenomenon. For contributions that fill gaps in scholarship and overturning social norms once set in stone, the narrative is necessary. The information in this book will fill a gap in the works of a number of scholars. I remain in contact with three Rosenwald scholars, who consistently keep track of the book's progress and publication for a variety of scholarly and personal reasons. The impact of this title is sheer excitement.

The development of the content was all in divine order. In fall 2011, I ventured to Fisk University in Nashville, Tennessee, where I processed the Samuel Leonard (S. L.) Smith collection. Smith was the director of the Southern office for the Julius Rosenwald Fund Library Program. During the review section, I came across a number of boxes stuffed with folders marked *libraries*, *library program*, and *book sets*. I was baffled as I had yet to read about a library program formed by the Rosenwald Fund. I searched the internet and various journals with my doctoral committee members, who were also not familiar with it. Though I had previously focused on Carnegie libraries, I knew I needed to make this contribution to the LIS field and beyond. The narrative is based on historical research present in the various philanthropic levels that the Julius Rosenwald Fund Library Program invested in the education of African Americans. Rosenwald, former president of Sears, Roebuck and Co., desired to improve "the well-being of mankind" through access to education. A number of Southerners are familiar with Rosenwald as the founder of the Julius Rosenwald Fund that established more than 5,300 rural schools in 15 Southern states. Though many publications focus on Rosenwald's contributions, none offer a comprehensive study of the library program. Once Julius Rosenwald recognized that rural schools were invalid without proper libraries, the landscape of literacy in the South began to change. The Julius Rosenwald Fund Library Program established more than 10,000 school, college, and public libraries, funded library science programs that trained African American librarians, and showed that libraries should be supported by local governments. The library program pushed to make drastic improvements in literacy within the African American community but ultimately enhanced the literacy and educational opportunities for the American South.

The book is organized by six chapters, ordered so that current and future scholars can further investigate case studies of philanthropic efforts to provide access and services to underrepresented communities. Chapter 1, "The Denial of Knowledge," details the systematic refusal to elevate a culture that contributed their lives to America. The chapter provides an overview of public library histories in America with a focus on how the North progressed much quicker than the South due to racism. It is the foundational chapter that introduces philanthropy in Southern libraries and the man for whom the book is written, Julius Rosenwald.

Chapter 2 provides the reader with information on the Julius Rosenwald Fund, Rosenwald's relationship with Booker T. Washington, and the monumental school-building program that starts the philanthropic campaign. It also sets a theoretical framework for the remaining narrative. The section "Library in the Life of the User" advocates for research in the LIS field with emphasis placed on the user, while "sense of place" and "life in the round" theories concentrate on sense of community applied to African Americans in the early 20th century.

Chapter 3 formally introduces the world to the Julius Rosenwald Fund Library Program, noting the different types of libraries funded and library services offered. The review is not limited to African American libraries and reading rooms, as the fund extended services to white libraries too. In addition, notable library figure Florence Rising Curtis is highlighted, along with her work coordinating significant portions of the library program. She is depicted, appropriately, as a professional of integrity and courage when the reading ability of African Americans in the South was demeaned.

Chapter 4 stands on the soapbox for the LIS field and discusses the struggles of black professionals to be recognized as such. It focuses on the education of black librarians and the ongoing theme of philanthropic financial assistance needed for measurable progression. The Hampton library science school is organized with financial assistance from major philanthropic organizations, most prominently the Rosenwald program. Here we see six case studies of HBCU libraries, the development of financial support, and a quantitative review of progress. Many HBCUs were teacher training schools that lacked the proper children's literature in their libraries, if there was even a dedicated facility. The collaboration with other organizations is also described as a means to scratch the surface of the fund's influence on other organizations.

Chapter 5 extends beyond the library program and gives more insight as to how the fund continued to invest itself in the black community beyond the founder's death. The fund and its board of trustees slightly shifted gears from schools to fellowships and scholarships, healthcare and medical service, library services, education, social studies, and race relations. This chapter also encourages scholars to discover and synthesize case studies that cross these disciplines as they historically relate to African Americans, particularly the health services on which the fund focused.

Chapter 6 takes a deeper look at the way Rosenwald anonymously provided financial support. This chapter explains not only his devotion to Jewish culture and subsequent unrecognized giving but also his beliefs about public giving and organizations not existing in perpetuity. This is challenged as a perpetual endowment greatly helped the fund to meet commitments after the economic crash. The chapter ends with recognition that philanthropy toward underserved communities is a form of social justice, one in which various organizations should seek to uplift all.

This is the untold story of the Julius Rosenwald Fund Library Program.

Chapter One

The Denial of Knowledge

DEVELOPING THE AMERICAN PUBLIC LIBRARY

Libraries provide free access to knowledge that can lead to progress in an individual's life. The public library acts as an open schoolhouse that teaches and gives to people of all ages, genders, economic statuses, and educational backgrounds the knowledge, recreation, and inspiration for that environmental adjustment called education.[1] Early 18th-century leaders understood the importance of access to books and acknowledged that various forms of education would be the key to producing good citizens. However, the earliest books in America were rare and expensive to acquire. At that time, books in the home mostly belonged to the wealthy and members of the clergy. With such limited access, the subscription library was naturally established. Benjamin Franklin and the Junto, a philosophical association, initially developed the concept of the subscription library. This library later evolved into the Library Company of Philadelphia in 1731.[2] Though the subscription library was open to the public, a membership fee or special authorization was required to gain access. The Junto became the blueprint for the "members only" social library.

Allan Ramsay is recognized as the first owner of a formal circulating library, renting his books in 1725. William Rind followed Ramsay in 1762, credited as the first American to circulate materials for profit.[3] Many progressive library developments occurred in communities of Boston, Massachusetts, where local leaders sought a new type of social library. They wanted to establish a specialized library that would cater to a specific audience or discipline. In 1807, the Anthology Club of Boston founded the Athenaeum Library. To date, it remains active and is recognized as one of the oldest independent subscription libraries. Boston's community leaders continued this trend when they sought to establish another subscription library. This time, the library would promote virtuous habits among young men engaged in mercantile pursuits and their desire for knowledge. The ambitious desires of the city's leaders were fulfilled in 1820 with the establishment of the first two mercantile libraries accompanied by the Mercantile Library Association.[4]

School libraries also played an important role in bridging the gap of access, first appearing in New York prior to the Revolution, servicing students and occasionally the community. One could reasonably argue that church and parish libraries, which serviced their congregations and the community, were the first free public libraries, though not tax-supported. These libraries later donated their collections consisting of materials on religion and theology, both public and private, to Southern college and university libraries including historically black colleges and universities (HBCUs). The recipient schools were often teacher colleges. Though a generous offering, it was not the children's literature necessary for the development of schoolteachers.

The idea of local, tax-supported public libraries took more than a hundred years since the Library Company of Philadelphia to be actualized. Though New Hampshire opened the Peterborough Library to the public in 1833, it was supported by the state's literary tax. Still, this was significant progress toward establishing provisions for locally supported libraries. These same provisions would help Boston support its continued ventures in literacy. In 1854, the Boston Public Library became the first public library supported by local taxes.[5]

LIBRARY DEVELOPMENT FOR AFRICAN AMERICANS IN THE NORTH

The North made rapid progress in establishing public school systems as well as libraries during the post-slavery and Reconstruction eras. This progression included schools and libraries exclusively for African Americans. Wilmington, Delaware, was one of the earliest communities where blacks strongly sought educational opportunities to better their lives. Quakers opened a school for Wilmington's blacks in 1798, and later in 1816 the African School Society opened another school exclusively for blacks. According to an 1837 survey, the school established was the only school for African Americans operating at that time.[6]

Philadelphia was another progressive Northern city related to library development for African Americans. In 1828, the Reading Room Society, consisting of free African American men, was formed to educate blacks in the area.[7] The literary society opened the first social library for black men in Philadelphia. In addition, as a response to the exclusion and their need for intellectual activity, free African American women of Philadelphia established the Female Literary Society, which was the first social library for black women.[8] The enlightened city also established the Philadelphia Library Company of Colored People in 1833, later incorporated in 1836, to serve the black community as the initial Library Company of Philadelphia had done for the white community. The literary society provided a place of learning and intellectual exchange as it built a collection that would educate its members on literary and scientific subjects. The society also promoted literacy and public speaking among its members.[9]

In a similar manner, other cities began to follow the examples of private literary societies. Baltimore's Enoch Pratt Free Library and its first four branches introduced service to users of all races in 1886 as a condition of Enoch Pratt's financial gift.[10] The North also led the way in library development by having African American leaders and administrators. Edward C. Williams (1871–1929) became one of those great leaders. As the first African American to be educated formally in library science (New York State Library School, 1900), he worked as a librarian at Adelbert College and later became the first African American director of the Howard University Library System.[11] During this progressive time of library development in the North, the postbellum South was limited by customs such as segregation that crippled its development.

GAINING ACCESS: AFRICAN AMERICANS AND SOUTHERN PUBLIC LIBRARY HISTORY

In the South, the development of library facilities for whites reflected the pace of library service to blacks, which was delayed beyond necessity. For instance, *Plessy v. Ferguson* (1896) legitimized Jim Crow laws and created a home for social customs that hurt the South's development. For African Americans, facilities and services were far from equal. During a time of limited economic development, separate facilities for the two races placed a greater tension on states' restricted financial resources for library appropriations.[12] The inadequacy of library provisions, social customs, and psychological factors caused handicaps that affected the progress of all black institutions.

A common misconception among Southern whites was "black development had to proceed, if at all, at a respectful distance behind white development."[13] This was a destructive attitude for the long-term oppression that affected not only blacks but also the entire Southern region. The rural South was a place where even the white residents had limited access to public schools and libraries. The underdevelopment of those institutions was a reflection of social, economic, and political trends of the region. According to

Barker, the multiple factors that influenced development in the South included the low per capita wealth, large rural population, unprofitable system of farm tenancy, social deterioration, the large black population, the expense of segregated public facilities, and mass migration from the region. He argued that the South had used its deficiencies as an excuse and defense mechanism for continuing in such a fashion. The region could have seized the opportunity to use those counterproductive factors as motivation to develop creative ways of increasing wealth and establishing higher standards.[14]

Neither structural nor social development was progressive for Southern states. Records of library service to blacks in the South prior to 1900 are nonexistent; rather, progress began in the early 20th century when a number of Southern libraries introduced service to blacks. These services were provided in segregated branch libraries or restricted sections within an integrated library branch. Commonly restricted services at many integrated branch libraries involved denying blacks access to reading rooms and the privilege of browsing in the stacks of circulating books as well as preventing blacks from withdrawing books from the library.[15] Other integrated libraries, such as the Lexington Public Library in Kentucky, established a segregated section. Prior to opening in a newly constructed Carnegie library, the library officials set up a colored reading room so African American patrons would be able to check out books.[16] Slowly over time, segregated facilities became preferred over integrated libraries.

At the turn of the 20th century, the South began to experience a boom in the development of libraries exclusively for African American users. One of the earliest examples was the Cossitt Library of Memphis, Tennessee. An agreement between the library and the Lemoyne Institute, a school for African Americans, established a library in 1903 dedicated to serving blacks. In the agreement, the institute furnished the room, while the Cossitt Library provided a trained librarian and freely accessible books to all blacks in Memphis. Another great example of progress in library service for blacks came from Charlotte, North Carolina, where the Charlotte Public Library for Colored People was established in 1901. Charlotte passed a tax earmarked for a Carnegie public library, making it the first known city to build a library for blacks from its own funds.[17] It is the earliest example of an independent black library. The library operated under the local government until 1929 when it became a satellite branch of the Carnegie Public Library. This collaboration served as a means to comply with regulations under the Julius Rosenwald Fund Library Program. The library would later participate in the Rosenwald County Library demonstration, providing a momentous example of service to African Americans.

In 1904, the Rosenberg Library of Galveston, Texas (a private institution), followed suit with special developments that included a board of directors and a separate branch for African Americans that opened for service the following year. Also, the board of directors built an addition to Central High School, making it the first structure with the sole purpose of providing quarters for a public library to be used exclusively by African Americans. Another notable development in Southern public library service for blacks was the Louisville Polytechnic Library (now the Louisville Free Public Library System) in Louisville, Kentucky. After being denied access to the library, Albert E. Meyeek initiated multiple conferences with the Louisville Library Board to express the necessity for a library that would exclusively service blacks. Meyeek captured the attention of director William F. Yust, who believed that "reading skills and access to books were paramount in the scheme for racial advancement."[18] Prior to 1896, Southern library segregation was caused by racism more than legislation. With the influence of Yust, the board decided to open the monumental Louisville Free Public Library in 1908. The Western Colored Branch (WCB) was then added to the system, which was the first public library in the nation to provide library services to the African American community using an African American staff.[19] This made the WCB the first black Carnegie public library. Houston, Texas, provided a similar example. During the year 1909, a group of middle-class African American citizens opened a library branch using only a classroom at a local high school. The group formed the Colored Carnegie Library Association and requested funding from the Carnegie Corporation for a better facility. With the support of Booker T. Washington and local white leaders, Carnegie agreed to open a new library facility in 1913 to service African Americans.[20]

With the development of the National Association for the Advancement of Colored People (NAACP) in 1909, the nation had an organization dedicated to gaining and preserving civil rights for African Americans. This organization consisted of blacks and whites, proving that the two races could work together successfully for the greater good and going against the historic *Plessy* decision. The NAACP attracted the attention of many philanthropists and various levels of government, which led these groups to join the cause for uplifting the African American culture. These organizations and philanthropists provided funds to a variety of educational efforts, including library services and facilities for African Americans.

PHILANTHROPY FOR SOUTHERN LIBRARIES

From the onset of slavery conquering the rural area, the South was poised to become dependent on a morally improper way of life that would forever hinder an entire culture. Though deemed the progressive era, progress in the early 20th century was slow in the region that needed growth most. The turn of the century was met with a murky, unstable, economic and social embarrassment as well as extremely limited educational opportunities for both blacks and whites. It was no surprise that the development of libraries paralleled that of the school system in the South, scarce and revolving around the farming season. Segregation was the destructive social norm, and the construction of libraries would contribute to solidifying, as well as eventually dismantling, the "separate but equal" falsehood.

The progressive era garnered a number of collaborations between Northern businessmen and Southern states, especially for the iron and steel giants that sought to not only spread their influence but also increase opportunities for the people. One of the initial investments that many businessmen, charitable organizations, and philanthropists looked to cultivate was education. With this highlight on the matter and financial power, major progress was made in the area of public schools, colleges, and community libraries.

Library service for all rural inhabitants of the Southern region was not provided at effective levels until the early 20th century. Much of this growth was due to aid from philanthropists and comunity foundations. They pushed city and state officials to provide and retain better-trained leaders of both races who possessed the ability to carry out experiments that demonstrated sufficient means of promoting education and library service with limited funds. With the skills to operate under restricted funding, better leaders could build and equip modern schoolhouses with provisions for a library. A number of wealthy businessmen and philanthropists with interest in developing the South served as allies to educators and politicians to provide millions of dollars toward the support of African American educational, cultural, and social institutions.[21] For the black community, provisions for educational institutions were slower than that of rural whites, including the development of branch libraries that exclusively serviced blacks due to the complete denial of access to the main branch. Thus, library access was limited; it was also often the only opportunity for growth, as such facilities would provide free access to books and socialization.

One philanthropist who raised awareness concerning the necessity of library facilities was iron and steel industrialist Andrew Carnegie (1835–1919). The mogul held an emotional investment through funding libraries across the South during the late 19th century through the early 20th century for both blacks and whites. His support for libraries stemmed from his own experiences as a young immigrant growing up in Pittsburgh and his certainty that libraries are equally important on the levels of education and culture.[22] One dares to say that Carnegie recognized the library as place far before that concept became commonplace. After all, libraries proved to be a way to provide cost-effective educational opportunities to those who could not afford formal education primarily due to an unrealistic financial burden attendance would impose. Carnegie managed to fund nearly 1,700 public libraries in the United States to the tune of more than $40 million.[23] He acknowledged the luxuries the library provided, how this lack of library facilities plagued the nation, and that libraries would contribute to more life opportunities. This was a possible remedy with strong potential to affect individuals and thus the country. After all, it was Carnegie who donated $350,000 toward building the country's first desegregated public library in Washington, D.C., in 1903.[24] The nation's capital was more than receptive to opening a truly public library; however, Carnegie would not immediately gain this response in the South.

While blacks were eager to use free public libraries as an avenue to education because the school systems were inadequate, other Southern taxpayers were not as eager or were outright opposed to blacks having access to libraries for fear of forced racial integration.[25] Despite knowing that the black schools lacked libraries and/or were not supplied the same level of resources as for whites, there were residents willing to resist complete access due to the inevitable encounter that would eventually take place. Researchers can deliberate whether the steel giant had no choice but to eventually offer funding for segregated libraries, or if he simply sought not to go against the Southern grain in efforts to provide access by any means. However, the fact is that once funding was granted, the city and ideology of individuals in power administered the construction of public libraries. The city met the stipulations to gain funding, including providing the land and commitment to support the library in perpetuity. Land ownership and long-term financial support were major obstacles, and perhaps even impossible, for blacks in the South. Black taxpayers would take years to campaign for the establishment of a black public library, independent of city funding.

Atlanta, Georgia, is arguably one of the most progressive cities today; however, it took decades to provide public library access to its black taxpayers during the early 20th century. Post Civil War, the city was focused on providing library service—but not to all. The efforts began with a bank teller, Derwin Jones, who collaborated with a number of acquaintances to establish a subscription library during the summer of 1867. Though access was advertised as free, it was not actually free of charge. In fact, membership was exclusive to white men until 1873 when they began to accept white women as members, committing to literacy for whites, not blacks.[26] This contributed to disparities in the class system embedded in Georgia's clay and highlighted the continued social injustice toward blacks.

A shift began in May 1889 when Carnegie donated $100,000 to establish the Carnegie Library of Atlanta, a public library. Considering the appropriated funds met Carnegie's requirements, in addition to another $45,000 he also granted to the city, the stage was set for library equality.[27] In March 1902, the long-anticipated library doors were held by a bright red ribbon during the opening ceremony. It was a wonderful day that only was overshadowed by the denial of access to all the city's African American, tax-paying residents.

Even though the public money that supported the Carnegie library grant was green, access was white only.

Despite blacks consisting of at least one-third of the city's population of tax-paying citizens, they lacked representation on all accounts including the library board. A number of African American community activists, including W. E. B. DuBois, often pointed out how unfair it was for the city to use monies from blacks only to exclude them in the most prominent public accommodation. As a trade-off, a separate branch was offered for blacks. Great, the black community would have access, right? Here is where the legacy of separate but equal reappears as factual. Carnegie made a separate offer of $10,000 for a colored branch, and while the black community in Atlanta continued to contest for an adequate library, the Carnegie Library of Atlanta's board and city continued without the proper enthusiasm for an adequate segregated (black) branch.[28] For nearly 20 years, access was denied to black taxpayers. The black branch in Atlanta would not actualize until 1921. Much credit has to be granted to Tommie Dora Barker, who had become the librarian for the Carnegie Library of Atlanta in 1916. She successfully solicited an additional $25,000 from the Carnegie Corporation, leading to the opening of the city's first free public library for African Americans in July 1921, and she established representation with the Negro Advisory Committee.[29] For 132 forward-thinking Southern municipalities that pursued library equality, they boasted 144 Carnegie libraries by 1917.[30] While some were integrated, others honored the South's tradition of segregation. Yet, by any means access was granted.

There were a number of local efforts supporting the establishment of Southern libraries. Individuals, religious and nonreligious organizations, and other educational institutions stepped in to fill a gap left by the local school system. One of the most determined was Faith Cabin Libraries. Named after the blind hope held by the founder of the movement, William Lee Buffington, and those invested to provide books to a newly built Rosenwald school for African Americans, Faith Cabin Libraries was one of many successful community works.

Buffington, a pastor, millworker, and South Carolina native, was solicited by Principal Euriah Simpkins to dedicate the schoolhouse. He immediately noticed the absence of books and began to rectify this matter. Lacking the financial means, he wrote to others, including Reverend L. H. King of Harlem, New York. King and his congregation held book drives for the Southern school and sent 1,000 books to Buffington.[31] The abundance of books led to a surplus that the school itself could not hold. With a community commitment to supply timber and provide transportation to the sawmill, the pursuit of a freestanding library began. December 1932 was met with a new log cabin–style library facility on the grounds of the school. The contribution to increase literacy in the region was welcomed with much praise by the local community and charitable organizations that were inspired to donate more books to the cause. There were enough books for the construction of more Faith Cabin libraries. This was truly a community effort as landowners supplied more timber for a second library, in addition to the county board of education adding to the lumber pile. The Federal Emergency Relief Administration provided labor for construction as well—rightfully so, as the need for reading materials for African Americans in the South was indeed a national emergency that was remedied mostly by nongovernmental and community organizations.

The South Carolina library movement was extended to Georgia with a total of 107 black communities benefiting from the availability of reading materials, free of charge.[32] Some of the libraries were housed in designated reading rooms, while the majority of the schools were housed in stand-alone structures, cabin style. This movement witnessed steady growth until the onset of the 1950s where it eventually ceased except for the progressive integration of public libraries and the consolidation of small public schools that held Faith Cabin collections. The Library Service Act of 1956 also assisted in providing more reading materials throughout the rural areas. The legislation, passed in June 1956, "authorized a maximum of $7.5 million a year in federal funds to enable states and territories to extend and improve public library services in areas with less than 10,000 population," resulting in 288 bookmobiles, approximately 800 new staff to state library agencies, and various types of library systems.[33]

PROPHET OF THE SOUTH: JULIUS ROSENWALD (1862–1932)

Julius Rosenwald and fund officials would recognize and rectify the literacy gap by creating a monumental library program for the American South. Born on August 12, 1862, in Springfield, Illinois, Rosenwald dropped out of school in his early teens to work odd jobs in New York City. He held multiple jobs simultaneously, including handling baggage for travelers and pumping pipe organs for Protestant churches. Only receiving 10¢ per hour, Rosenwald often argued that the amount of income did not matter as much as a person understanding the importance of saving.[34] This mindset stood the test of time and experience as he maintained a purpose for his savings. By age 17, he had entered the business world in New York City. He remained active there until 1885 when he became president of Rosenwald & Weil clothing manufacturers in Chicago. As a leading supplier to Richard Sears's mail-order business Sears, Roebuck and Co., Rosenwald greatly assisted in the planning for Sears's growth and expansion. In 1895, Rosenwald became an investor and elevated the company through the development of Sears's mail-order business. During this time, many people lived in rural towns and on farms. Lacking both private and public transportation made it difficult to travel into the city for shopping. This fueled business and allowed Rosenwald's fortune to accumulate to more than $200 million in the early 20th century.

Prior to his appointment as president in 1908, Rosenwald had served as the treasurer and vice president of Sears. Under his leadership, the company's revenue multiplied more than 100 times that of 1896.[35] Rosenwald maintained that a factor for successful business operations was ensuring each transaction had a mutual advantage to all parties involved (customers, employees, the company, and stockholders). The businessman was also the mastermind behind Sears's refund policy for unsatisfied customers. Under Rosenwald's guidance, Sears, Roebuck and Co. also established many programs beneficial to the company's employees, including the Employees' Savings and Profit-Sharing Pension Fund of 1916 for employees who served the company for a minimum of 10 years.

A born leader, Rosenwald devoted much of his time to working with philanthropic, educational, and civic organizations. For many years, he served as the president of the Jewish Charities of Chicago, chairman of the Chicago Bureau of Public Efficiency, and a member of the executive committee of the Chicago Plan Commission. In addition, he served on boards of the Rockefeller Foundation, the Baron de Hirsch Fund, Tuskegee Normal and Industrial Institute (now Tuskegee University), the University of Chicago, United Charities of Chicago, Hull House, the Art Institute of Chicago, and many other organizations. Rosenwald was passionate about philanthropy and helping those who could not help themselves. In 1910, he began to voice his concerns about the equality and social needs of African Americans. One of his initial philanthropic acts occurred when the Chicago Young Men's Christian Association (YMCA) made an appeal for aid to construct a YMCA branch for African Americans. Rosenwald offered to give $25,000 to any city toward the construction of such a facility. He required residents of both the black and white communities to raise $75,000 as a collaborative effort, and he emphasized that both races would be able to use the facility. Thirteen cities met the requirement for the 1910 offer, and in 1920 additional cities raised the money for a total of 25 Rosenwald-funded YMCA facilities for African Americans.[36]

In 1911, Rosenwald met renowned educator and author Booker T. Washington, and they quickly became close friends. He found Washington's work to be very impressive and admired him greatly. They remained friends until Washington's sudden death in 1915. Upon meeting Washington, Rosenwald accepted an invitation to visit the Tuskegee campus, where his interest in Washington, the Tuskegee Institute, and the students persuaded him to become a member of the board of trustees in 1912. This was a position he served diligently until his death.

Philanthropist and civic leader Julius Rosenwald (left) and Booker T. Washington, educator and political leader at Tuskegee Institute, February 22, 1915. *University of Chicago Photographic Archive, apf1-07303, Special Collections Research Center, University of Chicago Library.*

On his 50th birthday, Rosenwald confirmed his legacy as a committed philanthropist when he granted approximately $650,000 to a variety of charitable organizations. Among these gifts he provided $25,000 to Tuskegeee Institute to build schools near Tuskegee to be administered by Washington with a single stipulation: he required communities to match or exceed his gift.[37] One year later, Washington informed Rosenwald of the financial status of the gift. The communities had raised as much money as they could, matching all but $2,100. Washington and Rosenwald agreed to allocate the balance toward building six experimental, one-teacher-type (one-classroom) public schools for black residents. Rosenwald agreed, contingent on the schools' communities matching his gift, which was achieved with the help of Washington and community members.

The rural schools were built using the Tuskegee plans, which were designed by Robert R. Taylor, director of the mechanical industries program and staff architect of Tuskegee. The early designs were easily distinguishable from the later Rosenwald buildings as they reflected the Tuskegee-style curriculum intended for these schools, including space for industrial education, a small classroom for girls' domestic science work, and boys' vocational work in a separate shop building. The first school completed was the Loachapoka School in Lee County, Alabama, at the cost of $942. The African American community raised $150 toward the purchase of two acres of land for the site and also gave an additional $132 for the cost of labor. The white community contributed $360, and Rosenwald gave $300 toward establishing the first Rosenwald school.[38]

Washington dedicated each school during the spring of 1914 in the presence of the Alabama Department of Education state superintendent, state agents, and thousands of enthusiastic people—both black and white. Rosenwald was so pleased upon hearing this news that he granted an additional $30,000.[39] The extra aid went toward building 100 more Rosenwald schools for blacks throughout the state of Alabama in cooperation with Tuskegee Institute and other city and state officials. The modest philanthropic effort would become one of the most effective school-building programs in the American South.

NOTES

1. L. Shores, "Library Service and the Negro," *Journal of Negro Education* 1, nos. 3/4 (1932): 374–80.

2. M. Wheeler and D. Johnson-Houston, "A Brief History of Library Service to African Americans," *American Libraries* 35, no. 2 (2004): 42–45. Accompanied by "Timeline in Library Development for African Americans."

3. K. Nipps, "Anne Shallus's Circulating Library," *Journal of Library History* 26, no. 4 (1991): 608–10.

4. D. Battles, *The History of Public Access for African Americans in the South; or, Leaving Behind the Plow* (Lanham, MD: Scarecrow, 2009); Nipps, "Anne Shallus's Circulating Library."

5. Battles, *History of Public Access*, 7.

6. J. Newton, "Black Americans in Delaware: An Overview," in *History of African Americans of Delaware and Maryland's Eastern Shore*, ed. Carole C. Marks, 2nd ed., 14–31 (Wilmington: Delaware Heritage Commission, 1998).

7. D. Porter, "The Organized Educational Activities of Negro Literary Societies, 1828–1846," *Journal of Negro Education* 5, no. 4 (1936): 555–76.

8. Wheeler and Johnson-Houston, "Brief History," 42–45.

9. Porter, "Organized Educational Activities," 560–61.

10. Wheeler and Johnson-Houston, "Brief History," 43–44.

11. Battles, *History of Public Access*. Now Case Western Reserve University in Ohio.

12. D. R. Lee, "Faith Cabin Libraries: A Study of an Alternative Library Service in the Segregated South, 1932–1960," *Libraries and Culture* 26, no. 1 (1991): 169–82.

13. L. Lamon, *Black Tennessee: 1900–1930* (Knoxville: University of Tennessee Press, 1977), 62–63.

14. T. D. Barker, *Libraries of the South: A Report on Developments, 1930–1935* (Chicago: American Library Association, 1936).

15. E. Gleason, *The Southern Negro and the Public Library: A Study of Government and Administration of Public Library Service to Negroes in the South* (Chicago: University of Chicago Press, 1941).

16. Battles, *History of Public Access*, 34.

17. Ibid., 29.

18. Ibid., 32.

19. "A Separate Flame," Louisville Free Public Library, accessed May 29, 2019, http://www.lfpl.org/western/htms/sepflame.htm.

20. Battles, *History of Public Access*, 35.

21. G. Bobinski, *Carnegie Libraries: Their History and Impact on American Public Library Development* (Chicago: American Library Association, 1969).

22. M. Lorenzen, "Deconstructing the Carnegie Libraries: The Sociological Reasons behind Carnegie's Millions to Public Libraries," *Illinois Libraries* 81, no. 2 (1999): 75–78.

23. R. Mitchell, "Andrew Carnegie Built 1,700 Public Libraries, but Some Towns Refused the Steel Baron's Money," *Washington Post*, April 9, 2018.

24. Ibid., 1.

25. C. Knott Malone, *Not Free, Not for All: Public Libraries in the Age of Jim Crow* (Amherst: University of Massachusetts Press, 2015).

26. "100 Years of Library Service," Atlanta-Fulton Public Library System, accessed May 30, 2019, http://afpls.org.

27. Ibid. See also M. Griffis, "The Segregated Carnegie Libraries of the South," *Aquila*, University of Southern Mississippi, accessed May 30, 2019, https://aquila.usm.edu/rocprofiles. The additional $45,000 was received via two additional grants, in November 1889 and March 1901.

28. Griffis, "Segregated Carnegie Libraries."

29. Ibid.

30. M. Fultz, "Black Public Libraries in the South in the Era of De Jure Segregation," *Libraries and the Cultural Record* 41, no. 3 (2006): 337–59.

31. Lee, "Faith Cabin Libraries," 172.

32. Ibid., 180.

33. M. Farrell, "A Brief History of National Support for Libraries in the United States," Presented at the International Federation of Library Associations and Institutions (IFLA) Conference, Washington, DC, June 29, 2012.

34. Fisk University, Special Collections and Archives, Samuel Leonard Smith Collection, box 11, folder 4.

35. Fisk University, Special Collections and Archives, Samuel Leonard Smith Collection, box 7, folder 5.

36. N. Mjagkij, "A Peculiar Alliance: Julius Rosenwald, the YMCA, and African Americans, 1910–1933," *American Jewish Archives* 44, no. 2 (1992): 585–605.

37. M. Hoffschwelle, *The Rosenwald Schools of the American South* (Gainesville: University Press of Florida, 2006).

38. Fisk University, Special Collections and Archives, Samuel Leonard Smith Collection, box 11, folder 4.

39. Hoffschwelle, *Rosenwald Schools*.

Chapter Two

Unveiling the Well-Being of Mankind

THE JULIUS ROSENWALD FUND

By the early 1920s, the school-building program was rapidly growing and succeeding in Alabama and beyond. Other state agents and superintendents took notice and became eager for Rosenwald to extend his aid to building rural schools in neighboring states. The correspondents recognized the long-term benefits to the black community as well as the region. Rosenwald also received a multitude of letters praising his successful efforts from officials and other philanthropic foundations concerned with the state of African American education.[1] Rosenwald received these messages with gratitude but often responded with a humble demeanor that celebrated the men and women who carried out the work. The philanthropist felt the administrators and teachers were more deserving than he.

In August 1917, U.S. commissioner of education P. P. Claxton called a conference with the Southern state superintendents and agents to be held in Washington, D.C. The meeting focused on a report detailing the state of African American education in the South. The report, commissioned by the bureau, was written by Thomas J. Jones and funded by the Phelps-Stokes Fund. Rosenwald also attended the meeting and was greeted with many congratulatory chats focused on his generosity in assisting the state of Alabama. He actively expressed the need for schools in the South, and attendees countered with the need for aid in other states. Rosenwald suggested the men establish a committee to draft general plans for the proposed enlarged program and submit the plans to him for consideration. Immediately, the men selected Jackson Davis, field agent of the General Education Board; James L. Sibley, state agent of Alabama; and Samuel Leonard Smith (commonly referred to S. L. Smith), state agent of Tennessee.[2]

The three-man committee made four recommendations: (1) the Rosenwald program should extend the school-building aid to other Southern states that had state agents paid by the General Education Board; (2) all buildings were to have well-designed modern rural school plans; (3) aid should be increased to $400 for a one-teacher school and $500 for a two-teacher or larger school; and (4) the program was to continue through the Tuskegee Institute. Rosenwald approved the report for extending the school-building program. On October 30, 1917, he incorporated the Julius Rosenwald Fund in Illinois for the "the well-being of mankind."[3] Because there were too many causes the fund could assist for the betterment of mankind, for one man or one organization to undertake all matters in need of financial assistance was unpractical. After careful consideration of all the worthy causes, Rosenwald and the fund officials agreed the maximum benefit would only be achieved by concentrating on four major areas: education, health, fellowships/scholarships, and race relations.

The lack of modern building plans for the rural schools became an immediate issue. The fund commissioned Fletcher B. Dresslar, professor of hygiene and schoolhouse planning of George Peabody College in Nashville, Tennessee, to survey the schools. He evaluated the schools and provided a report with recommendations on the design, which resulted in Rosenwald opening a Southern office in June of 1920 in Nashville. S. L. Smith was appointed as the general field agent and then later promoted to director of the Southern office. Rosenwald selected Smith because of his education and experience in schoolhouse planning, hygiene, and rural sanitation as an understudy of Dresslar. Smith also designed modern rural school plans, one-teacher to six-teacher types, in Tennessee. He was committed to being the point of contact for Southern state superintendents and agents of the 14 cooperating Southern states concerning all general information and budget requests for the school-building program. Soon after the announcement of his appointment, Smith visited the department of education in each of the 14 states to assist with budgets and applications for rural schools.[4]

As a facilitator, Smith designed and prepared blueprints, building specifications, and bills for every school type. These plans became known as the Community School Plans and were used in 1920–1928. Other schools not funded by the Rosenwald Fund, both black and white, also adopted the plans. By the philanthropic act of one man, a program destined to become the largest and most effective rural school-building program by a philanthropic agency began to affect the lives of many African Americans and whites in the South. This venture resulted in the construction of 5,358 modern rural schools with a pupil seating capacity of 663,795, located in 883 counties of 15 Southern states, and costing $28,424,520.[5] The school-building program closed on July 1, 1932.

The archival documents in the Julius Rosenwald Fund archives and the S. L. Smith collection revealed that the fund constantly received requests to expand the scope of aid beyond school buildings, teacher homes, and vocational buildings in the South. The focus was expanded after a discussion on school bus transportation surfaced. Public school authorities in the region did not operate any bus transportation to or from the rural schools. Officials knew the bus transportation was necessary for the successful consolidation and operation of associated African American schools and the county training schools. After this information was presented to Rosenwald in 1927, he granted experimental aid to sponsor transportation for county training schools in two Alabama counties. This experiment proved to be successful as it provided transportation for students to attend school regularly with less harassment. Subsequently, aid was extended for school bus transportation in participating Southern states in 1928.

In 1927, the fund initiated health and library programs in the South. The philanthropic organization established these programs in response to issues exposed by the school-building program. For example, the initial program unveiled the dismal picture of health conditions in Southern communities where mostly infants and school-aged children were affected. Rosenwald consulted Smith and instructed him to collaborate with official health agencies. The fund provided aid to employ black nurses associated with county health agencies as an effective means of improving the poor health conditions of blacks. The fund was reorganized in 1928, with former director and vice president of the Rockefeller Foundation, Edwin R. Embree, being appointed as president. Later, Rosenwald requested a budget for the health program. At the next board of trustees meeting, the budget was approved, making the health program for blacks official. The philanthropic organization contributed millions of dollars to improving the health of Southern blacks.

Smith encouraged Rosenwald to assist in providing more books to blacks in the South. Upon reviewing reports on the rural schools, it became apparent the schools lacked library books and did not have nearly enough textbooks. Commonly, children would have to share terribly worn textbooks. Rosenwald argued the purpose of the modern rural schools would be ineffective without the simplest learning tools: books.[6] Agents of the American Library Association agreed with Rosenwald on the dire need for books in the schools. However, they warned him against spending a grand amount of money on libraries for the schools without professionals. The teachers had no access to children's books during their training; thus, they were ill equipped to guide the students effectively without the proper use of a library. Rosenwald decided to provide experimental aid by giving 10 elementary library sets (book sets) to Rosenwald schools for each of the 14 cooperating states. He also gave aid, as an experiment, to five black teacher training colleges to establish modern libraries on their campus. The results of the two experiments led to the establishment of the Julius Rosenwald Fund Library Program in 1927. The library program, which will be discussed in greater detail, helped establish nearly 10,000 school, college, and public libraries.

During the 1928 reorganization, the fund transitioned from private to corporate giving. Rosenwald gifted 20,000 shares of his stock in Sears, Roebuck and Co., bringing his personal contribution to more than 200,000 shares of stock, which was then a market value of $20 million. He believed that everlasting endowments could easily become a hindrance to progress. Thus, he stipulated all funds allocated to the generation within 25 years of his death.[7] The board of trustees agreed with Rosenwald, took on the existing programs, and expanded the scope to include high schools, colleges, African American hospitals and health agencies, county library service in Southern states, medical services to persons of moderate means, and general social studies. The realization that the progress of any group or organization depended largely on creative leadership led to granting fellowships and scholarships to black and later white Southerners to develop their talents. As time passed, the fund felt it no longer needed to provide opportunities solely for African Americans, and it incorporated into the general development of American life. The philanthropic organization shifted its emphasis to being an active program in race relations.

The Julius Rosenwald Fund was not created to exist forever. However, the fund came to a close sooner than was expected due to the economic crash of the stock market. The Sears, Roebuck and Co. stock fell from nearly $200 per share to less than $10 per share.[8] The fund, determined to meet its financial commitments, limited the programs and concentrated more heavily on wielding influence through studies, publications, and consultation rather than allocating additional funds to other agencies. The board ended the larger programs in general education and social studies. With these changes, the organization met all of its pledges, cleared debts, and continued to help active programs during the Great Depression. The trustees followed the policy of expanding principal and income. The work of the Julius Rosenwald Fund came to a close on June 30, 1948, keeping with the wishes of its founder who died in 1932.

Officers of the Julius Rosenwald Fund intended to use all of its funding to advance the well-being of mankind. Through philanthropic efforts, programs that enhanced opportunities in education and health, made fellowships and scholarships available, and thoroughly examined race relations demonstrated that the answer to the "well-being of mankind" was (and remains) literacy. This mantra is something Rosenwald demonstratively believed: the library provides monumental contributions to its community and the users.

LIBRARY IN THE LIFE OF THE USER

In an era occupied by rapid growth of information technology and communication capabilities, the value of the library in the life of the user perspective has been overlooked. Due to this reality, there is a need to reinvent and reconceptualize the library in order to stay relevant. However, the library and information science (LIS) field must promote the importance of the library in the life of the user perspective through research. Traditionally, research in public libraries places more emphasis on the library and not on its users. Zweizig called for the profession to shift concept focus from the user in the life of the library to the library in the life of the user, which would allow for a greater understanding of the contributions public libraries provide to communities.[9] He advocated the need for research in the LIS field with emphasis placed on the user, noting there are key factors when conducting user-centered research including the affect or influence on the users being the central focus. In addition, researchers must carefully select a research perspective on the user. Despite the design of libraries as public service institutions at the time of Zweizig's call, there were only 15 studies available that explicitly explored public library users, and these studies did not fill the gap in LIS scholarship because they were library centered. The studies focused on the user in the life of the library perspective neglecting to address responsiveness to societal changes, reference to other fields, theory development, and measures of impact on human terms.[10]

Lange credited Zweizig for bringing clarity and a different conceptual framework and for upgrading the methodology and theory for exploring user-centered studies.[11] Many scholars were influenced by the works of Zweizig and decided to answer his call to produce user-centered research. Kronus conducted a study to predict patterns of adult library use through regression and path analysis, finding education, lifestyle, and urban residence to be principal factors as the best predictors. He also uncovered age to have an indirect effect, but only when education and family size were held constant.[12] Massey suggested that library users be segmented by benefits received from the library or library activities to include learning, entertainment, children services, and simply being a place to go.[13]

In a 1977 study, Zweizig and Dervin determined that traditional user studies must venture beyond identifying library users and their frequency of use. Naturally, researchers answered the call using a variation of methods. D'Elia developed a conceptual model based on the behavior of the library user that included Zweizig's top seven individual characteristics from his 1973 study and four additional variables concerned with the respondent's perceived relationship with the public library.[14] He found that public library users more than nonusers had the tendency to perceive the library as more accessible. Other key factors among library users were that the frequency and intensity of use was directly related to awareness of special library programs, and in-house use was related to using other libraries.

Another researcher to answer the call was Madden, who conducted a secondary analysis of a national lifestyle study focused on the activities, interests, and opinions of three user groups (nonusers, moderate users, and heavy users).[15] He found that library use was highly associated with general activity. Also, female nonusers were more likely to become users whereas male nonusers tended to respond to information provisions made for home improvement and automobile repair. In addition, his study revealed that most users identified themselves as moderate users, whereas only a small portion sampled were considered to be heavy users. Finally, he declared that medium-size libraries were more likely to have the ability and resources (human and machine) to satisfy the needs of the three user groups.

More recently, Wiegand discussed various restrictions the LIS field has placed on itself by focusing mainly on technology and not the user, as he argued the size of the field allows for a wider scope of research. The field's focus, too centered on biography, library expertise, and big library institutions, is void of analysis studies focused on the impact of collections and services on library users, as well as the ways in which users appropriated both.[16] He too advocated for LIS researchers to shift their perspectives from studying the user in the life of the library to include more about the role libraries play in the lives of women, children, minorities, and working-class people.

Wiegand's revealing research on the "Main Street Public Library" studies library use in the life of the user. Wiegand uncovered two aspects of the public library: (1) public space to demonstrate and teach social behaviors as well as responsibilities acceptable to the community, and (2) literary space through collections and services that offered models for successful living, problem solving, and an orderly life. Wiegand often challenged traditional assumptions about the American public library in the community, whereas traditional thinking and academic teaching has been grounded in a perspective that identifies the public library as "a neutral agency essential to democracy" also known as "the library faith."[17]

Wiegand presented the argument that the public library is essential to its local community for reasons other than library faith.[18] As discussed by Zweizig, there is need for a body of research that examines "the user in his complex information environment, explicit development of our theoretical concepts of information use, incorporation of the findings from a variety of related disciplines, and use of sophisticated and sensitive methodologies for the interpretation of data."[19] When this body of research is created and flourishes, the LIS field will have truly made progress in understanding the library user. This book answers this call by using the library in the life of the user concept to explore the impact of the Julius Rosenwald Fund Library Program on African American users. The research is user centered as it evaluates the benefits and influences caused by the program's creation and outreach, and the increase of library services to the African American community.

THEORETICAL FRAMEWORK

Understanding the role of the library in the life of the user can be enhanced by new research guided by theoretical perspectives from other academic disciplines including American studies. American studies researchers can assist the LIS field with gaining knowledge about cultural agencies and practices in American libraries. One theory cannot completely explain how the library functions in the life of the user, thus two theoretical concepts to inform this research study are used.

SENSE OF PLACE THEORY

To effectively examine the impact of the Julius Rosenwald Fund Library Program in the lives of African American users, it is necessary to examine the library users' emotional attachment to environments and places. There are multiple factors that influence how individuals perceive different environments and how those environments fit into their world. Sense of place theory is often referred to as an all-encompassing concept that incorporates other notions describing relationships between humans and spatial setting.[20] This includes values and experiences considering aesthetics as well as a specific feeling in a dwelling. The theory draws on how people interact with their physical and social environments by examining the way a place affects an individual's life, and the ways in which that person creates a sense of place. Key factors include the difference between settings and the sense of place, which is based on an individual's experience of them. Each factor is heavily influenced by our own contributions.

As explained by Steele, place has two aspects: (1) the particular experience of a person in a specific setting, and (2) the spirit of place as a combination of characteristics that give some locations a special feel or personality.[21] Place experiences may involve immediate feelings and thoughts including worldviews, occupational practices, a sense of accomplishment, a sense of enjoyment, and intimate knowledge. For example, Feldman investigated sense of place in a black, middle-class community in Birmingham, Alabama, and the struggle of a culture to rise above discriminatory practices common in the South. In depth, the author described how the long struggle-turned-victorious battle of the community in overcoming oppression helped to create a sense of accomplishment for then-current and future generations.[22] This study supports Rutgers Center for Green Building's *NJ Green Building Man-*

ual's declaration that place is a center of meaning where human emotion and relationships are emphasized.[23] Sense of place resides in human interpretation and experience. Specific places have become symbols of power, principles, and ideals. Such places have been used as points of protests and conquests, including libraries. It is important for the LIS field to recognize this *sense* and not lose sight of its importance as it relates to the library in the life of the underrepresented user.

Libraries seek to create a positive sense of place for all its users and serve as a facility where many have developed a sense of belonging. Public libraries often function as central institutions in the daily life of users within small communities.[24] When the majority of the users are minorities, the library contributes a greater sense of place due to discriminatory social customs. Decades beyond establishment, libraries focused on the educational, social, and cultural needs of local communities. This created a sense of pride as it provided a tool to overcome inequality based on race and culture. In a study on the 135th Street Branch Library in New York (now the Schomburg Research Center for Black Culture), Anderson investigated the role of the library in the lives of the user during in the Harlem Renaissance. During this prominent time, the library staff connected "writers and their readers using literary gatherings; between artists and their viewers with art exhibitions; and between playwrights, performers, and their audiences with theatrical productions."[25] This connection between the library and the community is a great example of creating a positive sense of place that resulted in the library being viewed as an institution for educational advancement, social meetings, and community gatherings.

Sense of place theory involves understanding how people develop place attachment and feel a part of a physical and social environment. This attachment is commonly grounded in a "community's cultural response to the environment's features, the role that a place plays in satisfying human needs, historical meanings and symbolism embedded in the location, and the possibilities for individuals and groups to identify with space."[26] The efforts of the 135th Street Branch Library staff to expand its services to more effectively assist its users created a positive sense for the community and embedded a lasting sense of pride. The standard libraries set to uphold and create positive experiences should be a social mandate as the library continues to develop into a place where people of different ages, backgrounds, and interests may visit with comfort and confidence and where their information and social needs will be met. Sense of place theory is appropriate for this book as it helps assess the values and feelings people associate with those libraries sponsored by the Julius Rosenwald Fund Library Program.

LIFE IN THE ROUND THEORY

Elfreda Chatman, a champion of theory development in LIS education, pulled components from various theories in other academic fields to explain the information phenomenon she observed in her field study. In her efforts to go beyond her studies in information poverty, she found weakness in the borrowed theories. Though each theory built on the previous one, she sought to build larger theoretical concepts. Through her research exploration, Chatman created three theories that greatly benefit the LIS field: information poverty, life in the round, and normative behavior.

In the early 20th century, African Americans were continuously subjected to harsh and often violent acts of racism. For this reason blacks remained within familiar environments. Thus, it was common for blacks to live guarded lives in their own communities. These communities were mostly established post-slavery and would not easily expand to welcome white outsiders. To understand the information-seeking behavior of those living in these black enclaves, one must first investigate the social behaviors within the restricted environment. Life in the round theory is the appropriate model to conduct such a task.

Life in the round theory was developed through Chatman's study of the social world concept of women in prison. She explored the ways in which the women refined their social world in order to survive prison, mentally and physically. The ethnographic research led her to interview 80 female prisoners, revealing that a life in the round helped to sustain a normative existence. As explained by Chatman, a life in the round "requires a public form of life in which general knowledge aids in small learning" and "certain things are implicitly understood."[27] It is composed of normal language, worldview, and codes. Understanding this form of life occurs when the information is clear enough to give sensible meaning to things. The residents are very much a part of this process as it is defined by their values. Members, also known as insiders, are not concerned with the outside world because it has little influence on the insiders' experiences. Social roles and group standards, or norms, are created and sustained by the insiders. Chatman presented six propositions that constitute the theory of life in the round:

1. A small world conceptualization is essential to a life in the round as it establishes and legitimizes others within that world and sets behavioral boundaries.
2. Social norms force private behavior to undergo public scrutiny, deciding whether behavior, including information-seeking behavior, is appropriate.

3. The result of establishing appropriate behavior is the creation of a worldview including language, values, meaning, symbols, and a context holding the worldview within temporal boundaries.
4. For most of us, a worldview is played out as life in the round. It works most of the time with enough predictability that there is no point in seeking information.
5. Members who live in the round will not cross the boundaries of their world to seek information.
6. Individuals will cross information boundaries only if there is a perception that (1) the information need is critical; (2) the information is relevant; and/or (3) life lived in the round is no longer functioning.[28]

Chatman argues that life in the round will have a negative effect on information seeking for everyday behavior, suggesting the best use for the theory's application will be as a strategy for examining social life. If there is no need for individuals to seek information from an outside world, it is because their social world is working just fine without doing so. The information theorist is referring to a specific type of information intended to respond to the needs of individuals within a specific social context. A life lived in the round is a taken-for-granted lifestyle that acknowledges everyday reality as routine. In contrast, it is also constraining as behaviors are judged by standards determined by those within the round.

Observing life as lived in the round is crucial to understanding information behavior in the small-world context. There are a multitude of research studies focused on information-seeking behavior and information sharing in the LIS community citing Chatman's theory. However, very few of those studies focus on the topic of Southern public library history as it relates to African Americans. Historical racism led to a culture of mistrust among black Southerners. The resulting African American culture does not readily trust outsiders and instead seeks information within its own small world. The theory of life in the round is appropriate for this study because it explores the overlapping information and social worlds associated with daily life experiences of disadvantaged groups. The theory assists the study in exploring information behaviors rooted within norms and attitudes of the African American community, which later became challenged when access to library services became the new normal. The theory was a good measure while analyzing the influence of the Julius Rosenwald Fund Library Program on minority users versus their small world order.

The conceptual and theoretical frameworks guided the research and validated the connection between the library and its users. Key theoretical perspectives used to investigate the role of the library in the life of the user include the creation of a sense of place through an emotional experience and examination of information-seeking behavior in a small social world context.

RESEARCH DESIGN

The study focuses on the Julius Rosenwald Fund Library Program, which was established to supply reading materials and financial support to libraries in rural schools, black colleges and normal schools, and communities. By thoroughly investigating the philanthropic efforts of this monumental library program, the impact on the libraries is revealed. Though the library program no longer exists, the activities of the Julius Rosenwald Fund are well documented. Studying the archives allowed me to conduct an exploratory, archival analysis of data previously collected. I made use of a codebook with preset and emergent codes to organize and sort the data. Through analysis of archival documents, I explored the impact of the program on Southern libraries and, consequently, the role of the library in the life of the African American user.

The research question, which conveys the need to acknowledge the impact of the Julius Rosenwald Fund Library Program on libraries established and/or funded by the charitable organization, is "How did the Julius Rosenwald Fund Library Program influence library practices at Rosenwald-funded libraries and other Southern libraries?"

This single question is loaded with many subquestions, including "What types of services were provided in school and college libraries?" "Were these libraries also for social use?" "Once library facilities and materials became free to all persons of the community, was the library able to provide various types of library services?" "How did the professionals evaluate the users' information needs?" "After evaluation, was there an expansion of services?" "If so, what types of services were offered?" "As the fund's involvement diminished and later departed the county libraries, was the quality of service reportedly maintained?" "How were the services funded?" "What became of the professionals?"

The answers to these questions are revealed through content analysis of archival data with use of coding. The findings from this study will be discussed in a subsequent chapter within the context of historical and sociological concepts to deepen the understanding of the role of the library in the life of the African American user and the impact of the Julius Rosenwald Fund Library Program. The rest of this chapter breaks down the study procedures for transparency and to inspire others to replicate the study in order to unveil the effort of other philanthropic organizations and programs.

RESEARCH SITE AND ACCESS

Archival analysis was conducted at the John Hope and Aurelia E. Franklin Library at Fisk University in the Special Collections and Archives department. Founded in 1866, Fisk University is Nashville's first institution of higher education and currently ranks in the top 20 percent of all liberal arts institutions in the nation.[29] It is necessary to provide a background on the preservation efforts of the institution as a way for the reader to understand why the small liberal arts college has such profound historical collections.

Prior to 1928, there had been little effort at Fisk University to collect and preserve materials by and about African Americans. With the arrival of Louis Shores in 1928 as librarian, the university embarked on a systematic plan to build such collections and house the materials separately in an adequate space. A year later, Fisk enlisted the aid of foreign dealers to provide works for its special "Negro" Collection, resulting in the purchase of 28 pamphlets and manuscripts documenting the early history of black domestic servants in Europe. By fall 1930, the institution had hired experienced and knowledgeable bibliophile Arthur Schomburg as curator of the collection. He immediately began to build a collection for Fisk similar to his own by acquiring a number of unusual and retrospective works. Simultaneously, through an agreement with the Southern YMCA Graduate School in Nashville, Tennessee, Fisk concentrated on collecting works on African Americans prior to 1865. The university also gathered materials on blacks in the West Indies and Africa, a large pamphlet collection, and two rare and priceless volumes that remain the choice items in Fisk's collection.[30]

Arna Bontemps, author, librarian, and a key figure of the Harlem Renaissance, became manager of the institution's library and the first black head librarian in 1943. Although his budgets were consistently meager, he was able to build the Special Collections and Archives department by gathering the papers of such black luminaries as Charles Waddell Chesnutt, Langston Hughes, John Mercer Langston, Scott Joplin, and W. E. B. DuBois as well as the archives of the Julius Rosenwald Fund. Bontemps hired professionals who began to process the growing archival and manuscript collections for use by scholars and researchers.

Today, the library continues to build on the tradition of maintaining the Special Collections and Archives department with the intent to collect, organize, preserve, and make available for scholarly use the official records of the university, the archives of other agencies and organizations, and the personal papers of prominent individuals. Preservation efforts ensure that researchers can explore African American history and culture as well as the heritage of Fisk University. The department houses primary and secondary materials preserved among the 200 manuscript collections, 30,000 books, photographs, and other items.[31] Scholars use the materials for theses, dissertations, books, articles, and films among other types of publications.

At the start of this research, I contacted Jessie Carney Smith, dean of the library, and gave a description of the study in order to gain permission to use the Julius Rosenwald Fund archives and the S. L. Smith collection. She graciously approved in August of 2013.

DATA COLLECTION

Special collections and archives provide researchers with primary sources of historical events deemed to have evidential and informational value. Such materials are crucial to historical research because they validate history. Many cultures have benefited from archival preservation, including that of African Americans. Due to the initial oppression of slavery and the subsequent struggles of Jim Crow, there have been countless historical research studies that focus on milestone eras in African American history with the assistance of archives.

Until the 1980s, "white libraries and archives generally showed no interest in collecting primary source materials that dealt specifically with black culture."[32] Consequently, African Americans, philanthropists, and various organizations that desired to preserve the history made the conscious decision to deposit their records in archives with a focus on black history and culture. African Americans also created or funded separate archives in an effort to retain control over personal documentation, presentation and interpretation, and the terms of access.[33] African American history continues to come alive through a multitude of archival and manuscript collections.

The data concerning the Julius Rosenwald Fund was collected and preserved through similar efforts for future research. To address the research question, I used three archival collections: the Julius Rosenwald Fund archives, which consists of two collections, and the S. L. Smith collection. I chose the archival collections based on the documentation of the fund's activities.

JULIUS ROSENWALD FUND ARCHIVES

The Julius Rosenwald Fund archives consist of three archival collections. However, this research study analyzes materials from the original collection as well as the second supplemental collection. The original collection documents the reorganized corporate fund, 1928–1948, and contains more than 150,000 items processed in 1969 occupying 560 archival boxes. The collection is arranged into five series: (1) correspondence; (2) reports; (3) manuscripts; (4) newspaper clippings, photographs, and scrapbook; and (5) fellowship and scholarships. The materials of the reorganized fund reflect the new directions taken by its officers who expanded aid to colleges for teacher training and African American leadership; fellowships for promising scholars of various disciplines; research on African American health and medical services; book subsidies for school, college, and county libraries; appropriations for social studies; and contributions to agencies and individuals working in the field of race relations.

Supplement 2 of the Julius Rosenwald Fund archives consists of 25 archival boxes holding materials documenting the private and corporate periods of the fund, 1917–1946. This collection was processed in the summer of 2013 and has been arranged into eight series: (1) biographical information; (2) correspondence with the board of directors, 1922–1934, and meeting minutes, 1917–1930; (3) correspondence with the board of directors, 1917–1930, and financial information; (4) correspondence with the Study on Trade Schools; (5) addresses, articles, manuscripts, and reports; (6) scrapbooks and newspaper clippings; (7) photographs; and (8) correspondence with the Rockefeller Foundation. In general, the archives of the Julius Rosenwald Fund document an organization and its efforts to assist the growth of the Southern region with a focus on its African American culture.

SAMUEL LEONARD "S. L." SMITH COLLECTION

Dr. Samuel Leonard Smith (1875–1956), more commonly known as S. L. Smith, wore many hats in his life, including administrator, advocate, architect, author, and educator. Through traditional hard work and determination, Smith established himself as a national leader and key innovator addressing schoolhouse planning, hygiene, and rural sanitation. In 1920, he was asked by Julius Rosenwald to direct the fund's Southern office in Nashville, where he revised community school plans and assisted the fund in establishing more than 5,000 rural Rosenwald schools and contributions to more than 10,000 libraries. With the establishment of the last Rosenwald school, the Eleanor Roosevelt School at Warm Springs (Georgia), Smith retired from the fund in 1937.

The S. L. Smith collection consists of 59 archival boxes divided into three sections: the Julius Rosenwald Fund materials, S. L. Smith professional materials, and collected materials. I focused on the first two sections during the research study. Within the Julius Rosenwald Fund materials (section 1), there are 12 archival boxes filled with materials focused on the activities of the fund. Section 1 contains correspondence from many prominent individuals in education and U.S. history including Julius Rosenwald, Booker T. Washington, Horace Mann Bond, Charles S. Johnson, President Franklin D. Roosevelt, and President Hebert Hoover. In 1948, Edwin Embree wrote a letter to Smith agreeing to send all Rosenwald files, library, and other memorabilia to Fisk University. Section 1 also includes a variety of newspaper clippings, photographs, publications, printed materials, reports, writings, and miscellaneous materials.

Samuel Leonard (S. L.) Smith (1875–1956). *Fisk University, John Hope and Aurelia E. Franklin Library, Special Collections, Samuel Leonard Smith Collection, 1869–2007, box 48, folder 5.*

Within the Smith collection's professional materials (section 2), there are 34 archival boxes filled with materials concerned with the professional career of Smith. The section contains an abundance of correspondence from prominent figures including Mary McLeod Bethune, Florence Curtis, Fletcher B.

Dresslar, W. E. B. DuBois, Charles S. Johnson, George Sullivan, and Fred McCuistion. The section has a wealth of manuscripts and publications authored by Smith focused on African American health, education, libraries, and national conferences.

DATA REVIEW

As previously stated, the Julius Rosenwald Fund archives consists of three archival collections, although only two of the collections were used in this study. I was already familiar with the S. L. Smith because I was the processing archivist for the collection during an archivist fellowship sponsored by the Institute of Museum and Library Services (IMLS). Thus, knowledge of this collection allowed me to go directly to helpful resources. Typically, when a researcher investigates one collection, he or she finds unexpected links to other collections not planned for the research. A time cushion of one month was built into the data review schedule to accommodate such an occurrence.

DATA ANALYSIS

Fidel and Maxwell found it best for data analysis to begin as soon as data collection begins.[34] Whereas Yin concluded that it is best to wait until all data has been collected to begin so the researcher does not focus on the small details but keeps the big picture in mind.[35] This research study greatly benefits from archival practices as the data has been collected, arranged, and preserved so I could immediately pull information relevant to the study. I employed content analysis of archival data focusing on the Julius Rosenwald Fund Library Program, following the design suggested by Yin.

CONTENT ANALYSIS OF ARCHIVAL DATA

Patton defined qualitative content analysis as any "data reduction and sense-making effort that takes a volume of qualitative material and attempts to identify core consistencies and meanings."[36] Hsieh and Shannon explained the method is for "subjective interpretation of the content of text data through the systematic classification process of coding and identifying themes or patterns."[37] Content analysis is essentially a coding operation involving the logic of conceptualization and operationalization.[38] I used inductive reasoning to identify important themes or classifications that emerged from the data. Through careful examination and constant comparison, I was able to provide descriptive and explanatory conclusions concerning the impact of the Julius Rosenwald Fund Library Program. The qualitative method of content analysis assisted me in providing an in-depth and insightful description of the library in the life of the user perspective and the impact of the Julius Rosenwald Fund Library Program.

CODING QUALITATIVE DATA

Coding involves destructing the data to examine the discrete parts for difference and similarities. The combination of data collection and interpretation of the data allows coding to become the basis for the analysis. To sufficiently and accurately analyze the content, I have created a codebook to sort and organize the data because the codes serve as a label for summarizing and synthesizing what emerges from the data during the analysis process.

The study reviewed various types of libraries funded by the Julius Rosenwald Fund and the impact that the agency's involvement had on Southern library practices. Four library types funded by the library program were identified: African American, rural elementary Rosenwald schools, high schools and colleges, and county libraries. The library types were used as preset codes. In addition, the study also used the geographic area and library practices as preset codes. Though the study focused on the Southern region (in general), I made note of provisions made in specific states for library services influenced or encouraged by the possible receipt of Rosenwald funding, if presented in the archival data. The chosen time period for the study is 1927–1947 as the Julius Rosenwald Fund Library Program began with the allocation of funds to elementary libraries in 1927, while the county library demonstration occurred 1929–1937. The additional 10-year frame allowed me to review data that may have presented additional long-term outcomes. Though I began reviewing with preset codes, it is always possible for new codes to emerge during analysis, that is, emergent codes.

VALIDITY AND RELIABILITY

Content analysis produces a high degree of validity due to the lack of intermediate steps between the creation of the phenomenon being researched and the analysis of the data. However, reliability is at risk as there is a single researcher studying the phenomenon. This should not disqualify the quality of research data. The concreteness of archival materials studied in content analysis strengthens the probability of reliability; the coding process can be repeated without limits.

Validity and reliability are criteria used to evaluate the quality of research in the conventional research paradigm. As an interpretive method, qualitative content analysis differs from the traditional in its fundamental assumptions, research purposes, and inference processes. Thus, the conservative criterion is partial for judging the research results of this study.[39] Taking notice of this issue, Lincoln and Guba proposed four criteria for evaluating interpretive research work: credibility, transferability, dependability, and confirmability.[40]

Credibility is the "adequate representation of the constructions of the social world under study."[41] The scholars recommended a set of actions that would assist improvement of credibility of research results, including prolonged engagement in the field, persistent observation, checking interpretations against primary data, and peer interviews. To improve the credibility of the analysis, researchers need to design data collection approaches that are able to sufficiently solicit the representations and create a clear process for coding to asserting conclusions. I extended the time period of the study beyond the ending of the county library demonstration for reasons of credibility.

The second criteria set is transferability, where the researcher's working hypothesis can be applied to another situation. The researcher is responsible for providing data sets and descriptions that are strong enough for other researchers to make judgments about the findings' transferability to different contexts. In this study, I identified preset codes with explanation of use.

The procedure for establishing dependability and confirmability is through appraisals of the research process and findings. Dependability is determined by checking the consistency of the study's process, while confirmability is determined by checking the internal logic of the data, the findings, the interpretations, and the recommendations. The materials that could be used in these assessments include raw data, field notes, theoretical notes, correspondence, coding manuals, and process notes.[42] I detailed the process so that the study can be duplicated using a codebook for organizing raw data and end interpretation. The four criteria were applied throughout the study.

LIMITATIONS OF THE RESEARCH

The goal of the study was not to see generalizability but instead to gain an understanding of a particular situation and its activity within important circumstances. There are few limitations to the exploratory research study. A major concern for content analysis of archival data is that the researcher cannot control collection, arrangement, or preservation of the data. For this reason, the researcher could encounter a gap in records, including data on experimental or demonstration libraries. Thus, the researcher must take this data at face value, keep this limitation in mind while analyzing the data, and report the gaps along with all findings. The focus of the research is on a single organization during a specific time period in one region of the country. The results cannot be generalized beyond that focus. However, to attempt transferability, there is potential for replication of the research study with a focus on other agencies and organizations dedicated to library development in the same or other geographic regions.

The John Hope and Aurelia E. Franklin Library, Special Collections and Archives, owns each collection through deed of gift. During archival arrangement and processing of a collection, archivists follow the deed of gift and rely on their professional training for necessary discretion. The collections selected for research are void of use and copyright restrictions. I am required to disclose, in the permission to use application, a description of the project and whether publication is intended. In consideration of research ethics, I followed procedures to access the collections.

NOTES

1. Fisk University, Special Collections and Archives, Samuel Leonard Smith Collection, box 42, folder 5.

2. Fisk University, Special Collections and Archives, Samuel Leonard Smith Collection, box 42, folder 5.

3. Ibid.

4. Ibid.

5. Ibid., documents detailing the fund's expenditures.

6. Fisk University, Special Collections and Archives, S. L. Smith Collection, box 11, folder 10.

7. Fisk University, Special Collections and Archives, S. L. Smith Collection, box 11, folder 4.

8. Ibid.

9. D. Zweizig, "Predicting Amount of Library Use: An Empirical Study of the Role of the Public Library in the Life of the Adult Public" (PhD diss., Syracuse University, 1973).

10. D. Zweizig, "With Our Eye on the User: Needed Research for Information and Referral in the Public Library," *Drexel Library Quarterly* 12, nos. 1/2 (1976): 48–58.

11. J. Lange, "Public Library Users, Nonusers and Type of Library Use," *Public Library Quarterly* 8, nos. 1/2 (1988): 49–67.

12. C. Kronus, "Patterns of Adult Library Use: A Regression and Path Analysis," *Adult Education* 23, no. 2 (1973): 115–31.

13. M. Massey, "Markey Analysis and Audience Research for Libraries," *Library Trends* 24, no. 3 (1976): 473–81.

14. G. D'Elia, "The Development and Testing of a Conceptual Model of Public Library User Behavior," *Library Quarterly* 50, no. 4 (1980): 410–30.

15. M. Madden, "Marketing Survey Spinoff: Library User/Nonuser Lifestyles," *American Libraries* 10, no. 2 (1979): 78–81.

16. W. Wiegand, "Tunnel Vision and Blind Spots: What the Past Tells Us about the Present; Reflections on the Twentieth-Century History of American Librarianship," *Library Quarterly* 69, no. 1 (1999): 1–32.

17. W. Wiegand, "Main Street Public Library," *American Libraries* 42, nos. 9/10 (2011): 46–48.

18. W. Wiegand, "Main Street Public Library: The Availability of Controversial Materials in the Rural Heartland, 1890–1956," *Libraries and Culture* 33, no. 1 (1998): 127–33.

19. Zweizig, "With Our Eye on the User," 55.

20. S. Shamai, "Sense of Place: An Empirical Measurement," *Geoforum* 22, no. 3 (1991): 347–58.

21. F. Steele, *The Sense of Place* (Boston: CBI Publishing, 1981).

22. L. B. Feldman, *A Sense of Place: Birmingham's Black Middle-Class Community, 1890–1930* (Tuscaloosa: University of Alabama Press, 1999).

23. *NJ Green Building Manual*, "Sense of Place: What Is Sense of Place?" 1977, updated May 2, 2011; http://greenmanual.rutgers.edu/newcommercial/strategies/senseofplace.pdf.

24. J. A. Hersberger, L. Sua, and A. L. Murray, "The Fruit and Root of the Community: The Greensboro Carnegie Negro Library, 1904–1964," in *Libraries as Place*, ed. J. Buschman and G. Leckie, 79–100 (Westport, CT: Libraries Unlimited, 2007).

25. S. Anderson, "The Place to Go: The 135th Street Branch Library and the Harlem Renaissance," *Library Quarterly* 73, no. 4 (2003): 383–421.

26. *NJ Green Building Manual*, "Sense of Place," 1.

27. E. Chatman, "A Theory of Life in the Round," *Journal of the American Society for Information Science* 50, no. 3 (1999): 212.

28. Ibid., 214.

29. Fisk University, John Hope and Aurelia E. Franklin Library, 2013, http://www.fisk.edu/academics/library.

30. J. Smith, "About Fisk Special Collections" (2009), Fisk University Library flyer.

31. J. Carney Smith, "From Andrew Carnegie to John Hope Franklin: Library Development at Fisk University," *Tennessee Libraries* 59, no. 4 (2009): 59.

32. J. Goggin, "Carter G. Woodson and the Collection of Source Materials for Afro-American History," *American Archivist* 48, no. 3 (1985): 261.

33. R. Jimerson, "Embracing the Power of Archives," *American Archivist* 69, no. 1 (2006): 19–32.

34. R. Fidel, "The Case Study Method: A Case Study," *Library and Information Science Research* 6, no. 3 (1984): 273–88; J. Maxwell, *Qualitative Research Design: An Interactive Approach*, 2nd ed. (Thousand Oaks, CA: Sage, 2005).

35. R. Yin, *Case Study Research: Design and Methods*, 3rd ed. (Thousand Oaks, CA: Sage, 2005).

36. M. Patton, *Qualitative Research and Evaluation Methods* (Thousand Oaks, CA: Sage, 2002), 453.

37. H. Hsieh and S. Shannon, "Three Approaches to Qualitative Content Analysis," *Qualitative Health Research* 15, no. 9 (2005): 1278.

38. E. Babbie, *The Basics of Social Research*, 6th ed. (Belmont, CA: Wadsworth/Cengage Learning, 2013).

39. J. Bradley, "Methodological Issues and Practices in Qualitative Research," *Library Quarterly* 63, no. 4 (1993): 431–49.

40. Y. Lincoln and E. Guba, *Naturalistic Inquiry* (Beverly Hills, CA: Sage, 1985).

41. Bradley, "Methodological Issues," 436.

42. Y. Zhang and B. M. Wildemuth, "Qualitative Analysis of Content," in *Applications of Social Research Methods to Questions in Information and Library Science*, ed. B. Wildemuth, 308–19 (Westport, CT: Libraries Unlimited, 2009).

Chapter Three

The Untold Story of the Julius Rosenwald Fund Library Program

Colonial America deemed the library to be the heart of a culture as it acted as a schoolhouse, freely offering people growth through knowledge. Thus, the library is the heart of grade schools, colleges, and communities. Yet library service was scarce in the South. In the rural region, most of the population lacked access, which was a major issue the region could not afford to ignore if it desired to produce good citizens and compete with the North for big business.

When discussing the activities of the Julius Rosenwald Fund, Southerners often mention Samuel Leonard (S. L.) Smith, director of the Southern office in Nashville, Tennessee. For more than 10 years, Smith was actively engaged in assisting Rosenwald with improving the rural schools. However, his influence went beyond the school building-program. In fact, it was Smith who encouraged Rosenwald to assist in providing more books to African Americans in the South.

THE LIBRARY OR THE LIBRARIAN

During a review of reports on rural schools, Rosenwald noted the schools' lack of library books and textbooks. Schoolchildren would often share exceedingly worn textbooks. Rosenwald argued that the purpose of the modern "Rosenwald" rural schools was ineffective without the simplest learning tools: books.[1] Agents of the American Library Association agreed with Rosenwald on the immense need for books in the schools. However, they warned him against spending a large amount of money on libraries for the schools without trained teachers. During the training, teachers did not have access to children's books, making the instructors ill equipped to properly guide the students to use the library. There was also an unjustified belief that African American children would not read despite the presence of library books. This theory was solely based on the assumption that black parents did not or could not read, so it was assumed that the children were not encouraged to do so. Despite this misconception, Rosenwald felt it necessary to proceed with overcoming the obstacle instead of concerning himself with whether the library or the librarian should come first. To brainstorm a sufficient solution, he consulted officers from the American Library Association, the Carnegie Corporation, the General Education Board, and the Jeanes and Slater Funds. A meeting of the minds resulted in the Hampton Institute (now Hampton University) Library Science School in Hampton, Virginia, for training African American librarians of school, college, and public libraries. This action later encouraged the founding of the Julius Rosenwald Fund Library Program as a cooperative program to develop library service for the rural south.

Prior to the Hampton Institute Library Science School, there was one library school in the South: the Carnegie Library of Atlanta Library School. However, the school only trained whites to become librarians. The Carnegie Corporation funded the school, from 1914 to 1925, until it agreed to provide the initial funding to organize and support the new school. Florence Curtis was appointed as the school's first director. She equipped the school with a trained staff, so the school could meet standards to be an accredited library school. After the Hampton library school opened, efforts were refocused on libraries for rural Rosenwald schools. With cooperation from Jackson Davis of the General Education Board and Alfred K. Stern, director of the Julius Rosenwald Fund's Chicago office, an effective plan was created.

RURAL SCHOOL LIBRARIES

In 1927, the fund gave experimental aid to purchase 10 elementary library sets in Rosenwald schools. Officers of the fund, state departments of education, and librarians acted as consultants for the project. Much time, thought, and devotion went into the selection of books for the smaller schools, including the county training schools. The team also put much consideration into the selection of library equipment and supplies, as well as general instruction on caring for and using the library. The list of books was approved by the Southeastern and American Library Association. Each library set contained up to 150 books and was purchased by Sears, Roebuck and Co. at wholesale cost. The fund paid for the cost of transporting the books as well as one-third of the cost to furnish the library, including necessary supplies.[2] The rural and public school authorities were required to pay for the remaining costs.

The elementary library sets were given to 10 Rosenwald schools per state. State agents selected counties with Jeanes Supervisors, who were African American teachers elected for their leadership qualities and "skill in teaching the industrial arts."[3] The teachers worked in rural schools and communities to educate blacks and were required by the fund to care for the library sets. The county superintendents were required to give necessary attention to using and caring for the libraries. They also agreed to furnish reports of the projects at the end of the school year. After the schools received the library sets, state officials and a librarian visited each school to give complete instructions on using and caring for the books, including record keeping and annual reports. The principal and all teachers were advised to read each book in order to sufficiently guide the students.[4] The following school year, 1928–1929, the fund doubled the number of library sets for each state. Eventually, the Julius Rosenwald Fund Library Program extended this offer to all rural schools that met the requirements.

AFRICAN AMERICAN COLLEGE LIBRARIES

Simultaneous to the experiment with the elementary library sets, the philanthropist agreed to grant experimental aid to five African American teacher training colleges. The five colleges were Agricultural and Industrial State College (now Tennessee State University) in Nashville, Tennessee; Southern University in Baton Rouge, Louisiana; Tuskegee Institute (now Tuskegee University) in Tuskegee, Alabama; Petersburg Normal and Industrial Institute (now Virginia State College) in Petersburg, Virginia; and North Carolina College (now North Carolina Central University) in Durham, North Carolina. Winston-Salem Teachers College (now Winston-Salem State University) in Winston-Salem, North Carolina, was later added as it trained teachers on a high level for elementary schools, while the other five colleges trained teachers for schools of all grade levels in the state.[5] At the time, none of the selected colleges possessed an adequate library. What the colleges considered a library lacked a librarian, an adequate building, modern equipment, and a collection of usable books to accommodate readers.

The Julius Rosenwald Fund Library Program granted each college library $1 for every $2 it raised, up to $2,500, on three firm conditions: the library must have a trained librarian and an adequate library building or reading room with modern furniture, and it must purchase books from a list approved by Curtis.[6] Each college agreed to meet the requirements and selected an exemplary teacher to attend the Hampton Institute Library Science School for a year of study, during the 1927–1928 academic year, which was sponsored by the General Education Board. During the school year, the selected teacher collaborated with Curtis to understand the needs of their college and to properly create a list of reading materials, modern shelving, and other equipment.

When the librarians returned from their studies, they were met by a completed library facility ready for use beginning summer or fall 1928. Most of the institutions' board of trustees exceeded the minimum financial requirement with the cooperation of the General Education Board, the Slater Fund, and enthused local citizens—rightfully so, as most African American institutions also served the surrounding community. The fund's library program extended aid to 43 black colleges and normal schools.

HIGH SCHOOL LIBRARIES

In an effort to continue library development, in 1929 the fund extended the library program to high schools. The match requirement had proven to be a great standard. Thus, the plan for the high schools would not greatly veer from the experiments. Any African American high school was eligible to receive $240 in aid toward the purchase of $720 worth of books.[7] A list of 1,000 books was prepared as a guide for the schools under the supervision of Jackson E. Towne, librarian of George Peabody College. To assist the schools in promoting proper use of the libraries, the fund agreed to cover

Erastus M. Cravath Memorial Library at Fisk University, September 7, 1930. This building was partially funded by the Julius Rosenwald Fund. *Fisk University, John Hope and Aurelia E. Franklin Library, Special Collections, Julius Rosenwald Fund Archives, 1917–1948, box 560, folder 1.*

expenses incurred by librarians while visiting the schools to instruct the teachers and students on the care of the library. Many of the school librarians in the state departments of education were also paid by the General Education Board as they devoted much of their time to developing white and black school libraries.

COUNTY LIBRARIES

In 1928, Rosenwald greatly increased the assets of the fund and secured Edwin R. Embree as president. Under Embree's direction, the scope of the fund significantly expanded. With the library program under way at rural schools and colleges, the fund decided there was still an immense need for library service in the rural South. Louis R. Wilson studied the then-current state of rural libraries, unveiling the fact that 71 percent of the South's population was entirely without library facilities and services.[8]

The library program, which had solely focused on school and college libraries, shifted its attention to developing county libraries. Rosenwald often demonstrated to fund officials the safety in starting a major project with experimental aid to ensure initial success. With the founder's guidance, officials decided to experiment with county demonstration libraries and appropriated $500,000 for a five-year period. Key principles for the demonstration were established for the long-term stimulation of Southern libraries. The selected libraries were to act as a "demonstrator" to other counties on the type of library service that should be provided to the community. The principles, tied to receipt of funding, required that all persons of the county—urban and rural, white and black—should have access to adequate, free library service; that the fund assist on a diminishing scale over a period of five years; that all the public library facilities of the county be under the direction of a trained librarian; and that the county provide suitable housing for the libraries.[9] In addition, the fund insisted on a minimum expenditure of 50¢ per capita for library service exceeding the national average. The fund required its traditional stipulation for funding, calling for the community to provide as much money as possible and obligate themselves to carry on the library service with the same standards after the fund departed.

Initially, the fund sought to grant aid to 2 county libraries in 13 Southern states. However, only 11 counties in 7 Southern states were assisted. For various reasons, the other states could not participate. Georgia and Florida were immediately disqualified because neither state had laws that enabled the counties to appropriate money for libraries. Virginia, Kentucky, and Arkansas were unable to meet the key principles set forth by the fund.

The Carnegie Corporation, which had a long interest in library service, contributed multiple grants totaling $200,000 in 1932 and 1933. This aid extended the county library demonstration two additional years without further obligation from the fund.[10] Carnegie's gift enabled the fund to continue without diminished effect. For seven years, community members of the 11 rural counties had the advantage of library facilities, literature, and adequate services. It was crucial for the libraries to be the boon of education and race relations in the developing counties that supported them.

RESEARCH FINDINGS

In anticipation of the findings, I noted a number of codes (preset) thought to provide a complete picture of the influence that the Julius Rosenwald Fund Library Program had on the lives of African American users by looking at the library practices provided in funded libraries. Specifically, I focused on four preset codes: library type, library practice, geographic area, and time period. Despite the preset codes, I remained unbiased so that emergent codes could freely surface. I used a codebook to organize the data. The findings of the archival study are given in detail below. This chapter examines the library practices at the Rosenwald-funded libraries. During data collection, I paid special attention to the archival documents that presented information on the fund's library program and the library practices.

PRESET CODE: LIBRARY PRACTICE BY LIBRARY TYPE

During the archival analysis process, it became apparent that the preset codes "library type" and "library practice" should be combined for a more cohesive presentation of the research findings. This was due to the collection's arrangement, which focused on the library practices and services each library type provided to its users. Otherwise, the findings would have much redundancy.

RURAL SCHOOL LIBRARIES

As previously discussed, the fund began its work in library development by supplying small libraries to the rural schools. It should be noted that in relation to the rural schools, the term "libraries" refers to a set of books or book collection provided by the fund. During the first year, 140 sets were ordered consisting of two different libraries: the original book collection and a supplementary book collection. The book lists were created after consultation with officers of the American Library Association (ALA); the head of the Hampton Institute Library Science School, Florence Curtis; and other library school administrators. The fund contributed one-third of the total cost and freight charges. The schools paid the remaining balance.

The archival collections used in the study—the Julius Rosenwald Fund archives and the S. L. (Samuel Leonard) Smith collection—held the outcome and success of the unsung library program. The collections document the determination of the fund's officials to provide libraries to the rural schools as well as the determination for the initial library experiment to not fail. They needed it to be a successful indication of what this program could do for the rural South. S. L. Smith was a key administrator who was emotionally invested in the library program. As the person who suggested the program to Julius Rosenwald, Smith strongly felt that an increase in literacy levels would greatly enhance the lives of Southerners. In a 1927 report, he reported the total of 400,000 volumes in Southern libraries that serviced African Americans. These titles were estimated to be valued at $1 each.[11]

According to documents in the S. L. Smith collection, the benefits of providing libraries to the rural schools greatly exceeded his expectations. The initial year, Smith traveled to many of the schools that received the libraries. The state agent and county superintendent accompanied him during the school visits. He asked each group of students four questions concerning the reading materials:

1. How many students have read one book?
2. How many students have read five books?
3. Who would like to name the titles of the books you have read?
4. Who wants to share their favorite story?

Each visit, students would eagerly raise their hands in response. All the students had read at least one book, while nearly "90 percent raised their hands" when asked who had read five books.[12] The students easily named the titles read and were eager to share their favorite stories, all much to the visitors' surprise as the teachers gleamed with pride. It was initially assumed the success was due to the experiment. It was later made clear that the eagerness was due to a genuine desire to read. As time progressed, the practices of the libraries and the students' eagerness did not fade or waver. The library practices were determined to be the cause of the successful experiment and the future of the library program.

The key library practice was educating the principals and teachers about the library. The educators were required to take a specialized summer course at a local teachers college on caring for and using the library. The course was under the direction of the state librarian and often the state's library field agent. The archival documents detail the library practices provided at the libraries. Most notable on the list is responsibility for the books placed in the hands of the principal. The head of the school was responsible for the complete library during the school session. However, he had the authority to appoint a teacher to act as the school librarian or custodian of the library set.

They would be charged with duties of record keeping, including circulation statistics and duly noting books added to the collection. [13]

Upon receipt of the library, the librarian and the staff were to prepare the volumes by entering each title on a separate line in the accession book. This ensured a permanent record of the book in the library. The library practice of record keeping assisted the librarian in documenting usage as well as user reading levels. The fund was sure to be strict on book preparation because it was essential for proper use.

Free access and use of the books is a library practice that was given special attention. The use of the library was a condition of receipt. The number-one condition to receiving a library set from the Rosenwald Fund was allowing all pupils, teachers, and community residents to access and use the books. The fund used this stipulation in efforts to improve literacy to enhance all opportunities in life. Access was step 1 to improving the lives of African American users. The next steps were teaching the users how to use and care for the library as well as the importance of the books. The students were given a lecture on the proper handling of a book, using bookmarks versus bending upper page corners, using book covers for preservation, and the need to keep the books out of reach of small children at home. [14]

Other library practices that allowed the rural school libraries to be successful were the consistent addition of new books and the service provided to community residents as well. The constant flow of new volumes contributed to the library's ability to service the community as well as the students serviced on a daily basis. In turn, the school library became an early form of the public library, as we now know it. Collection development was a major contribution to keeping the interest of the readers because the process considered readers on all levels. This helped to debunk the misconception that African American children could not read because their parents could not or would not read. In reality, there was not a lack of encouragement but a lack of supply. The Julius Rosenwald Fund encouraged reading by providing library facilities and books.

The circulation of books was another positive contribution for those not enrolled in school. The Julius Rosenwald Fund archives reveals the inability for all school-aged children to take part in school. Many were responsible for family farms or held jobs as maids and sharecroppers, which often prevented them from attending schools. The practice of circulation provided those not in school with reading material. Books were checked out for a two-week period, with one allowed renewal as long as they were kept in good condition. When a student took home a book, it was estimated that three other individuals also read the title. [15]

The library program required the principal or governing teacher to provide annual reports on the use of the library. The state agent and librarian who also visited the libraries filed reports at the end of the experimental year for every school. Each report noted that the average black student read as many books as the average white student.[16] The reports often recorded the level of circulation in the library and outside the library, taking into account the number of nonstudent readers. Due to such a strong desire for reading materials, the library remained in service during the summer months at a minimum of one day per week, using volunteers, parents, and trustworthy older students to operate the library. This was merely a teaser for the eager readers as they anticipated the new school term with hopes of exciting titles to conquer. Furthermore, the reports made it evident that books selected on various levels provided the users with healthy recreation and played a vital part in the reduction of juvenile delinquency.[17] Subsequently, a well-read individual made for an eager learner. The libraries were vital in producing better-educated individuals who became productive citizens.[18]

The library practice of "reading encouragement," as I have dubbed it, is a key component to the success of the Julius Rosenwald Fund Library Program. Teachers were taught to encourage students to gain and nurture healthy reading habits while young in an effort to increase their interest in all school subjects. It was understood that the test of literacy has two components: Can the student read? And does the student read? This concept behind reading encouragement is that whenever the pupil is taught to read and supplied with good, age-appropriate literature, discipline is much easier. This newfound discipline may also lead to increased attendance and a rise in the standard of scholarship.[19] Well-practiced teachers put life into their narrative by reading aloud with animation and by telling stories from a point of view that arouses curiosity in their students. This practice alone creates interest, as students will want to know the whole story. However, the practice would be ineffective if teachers were unfamiliar with the books in the library set. The fund deemed it necessary for all teachers and principals with access to the Rosenwald library to read all titles they are unaware of in order to sufficiently provide accurate reader advisory services to students as well as community users.

Due to the successful library practices at the rural schools, the fund saw fit to spread the benefits to white elementary schools. Ultimately, the elementary libraries created and enhanced the students and residents' appetites for increased reading materials. The Julius Rosenwald Fund Library Program established and contributed to more than 7,000 libraries to elementary schools.[20]

AFRICAN AMERICAN COLLEGE LIBRARIES

The Julius Rosenwald Fund archives provides an abundance of documentation on the college division of the library program, its development, and its

African American schoolchildren reading inside a Rosenwald school. *Fisk University, John Hope and Aurelia E. Franklin Library, Special Collections, Julius Rosenwald Fund Collection, supplement 2, series 7, photographs, box 24f.*

ultimate success. During the groundbreaking library conference held at the Hampton Institute on March 15–18, 1927, notable librarian and head of the African American branch of the Louisville Free Public Library, Thomas F. Blue, spoke about the library as a community center. It was at this conference that S. L. Smith became interested in establishing libraries in rural schools and teacher training colleges. Jackson Davis, field agent of the General Education Board (GEB), felt the distinct need for libraries of children's literature to be established for use during teacher education. He suggested to Smith that, during the next academic year, the fund select five colleges to aid in the purchase of books for children's literature library and a second library for the college itself. The cost of this assistance was to be distributed equally among the college, the Julius Rosenwald Fund, and the GEB. Davis also suggested the initial five institutions. These schools were in dire need of library aid, the administration was particularly interested, and plans for improvement were under way.

Though Rosenwald was interested in assisting the college libraries, he did not want to bear the responsibility of the program's finances and wished for the GEB to formalize their agent's suggestion. He also hoped for the Carnegie Corporation to bear one-third of the cost. Despite the lack of additional support, Rosenwald was not deterred. He did not allow their lack of action toward aiding black college libraries to stop him from assisting in developing black communities. He strongly felt the need for library aid to purchase books because the schools were doing all they could without additional aid, including an adequate library. Without adequate library service that included children's literature, newly trained teachers had completed an education program lacking any conception of a library for children. Yet, despite the lack of support, Rosenwald allowed Davis to make the offer to the selected five black colleges on his behalf without using his name or mentioning the Julius Rosenwald Fund, as he did not want the GEB to feel he was attempting to persuade them to make an offer of support. He wanted the officials to recognize the importance and need for the matter on their own, something the GEB never did, financially.

The initial offer to the college libraries to purchase a library of children's literature and an appropriate college library included Rosenwald's contribution of one-third of the cost between $500 and $1,000. Accordingly, the total cost could not be less than $1,500 and not exceed $3,000. The college was to acquire the required supplemental sum from other sources, which made it possible for the state department of education to apply for aid from other organizations including the General Education Board. The offer was set to expire December 31, 1927. As with rural school libraries, the books had to be selected from a list created by Curtis, who was also responsible for approving book purchases for each college. With the offer made to the experimental group, the college library list began to expand beyond grade-school literature as deemed appropriate, as college students were older and far more advanced than students in lower grade levels. Curtis, who had developed relationships among the college librarians and presidents, begin to draft the college library list based on the needs of the individual colleges.

To encourage a collaborative effort, fund officials sought the opinions of the head librarians at Columbia University and the University of Chicago to make contributions to the college list. However, racism would cause a rift in the relationship. In a 1927 letter, McKendree L. Raney, director of the libraries at the University of Chicago, wrote to Alfred Stern of the Julius Rosenwald Fund, saying the current list was far too advanced for "Negro students in the South" and it would be best to stick with a simpler list.[21] Beyond the elementary and high school titles, the college library list consisted of literature covering various collegiate majors such as physics, economics, anthropology, botany, German, English, history, education, and library science, among other disciplines.

Though Raney had taken no issue with the elementary and high school lists, he felt that the college portion needed a radical revision as he argued in the same letter, "These titles shoot over the heads of those who are intended to use them," and the list offered is on par with college courses offered at the University of Chicago, whereas black students of the South are nowhere near such standards, he assumed.[22] He advised that the list needed to be downgraded to the level of high school to match the black colleges' curriculum. This assumption was based on course offerings of many black colleges, which boasted college courses but also offered grade school or a college preparatory curriculum at the normal schools. Curtis would later correct his assumption with proof of consistent growth of the black colleges, including a 1926 study of 99 black colleges that revealed an enrollment of 13,000 black students with projected growth. In a passive-aggressive manner, Raney offered the services of discipline-specific professors from the University of Chicago to overhaul the current list and create a new bibliography. Needless to say, this correspondence created an issue with the fund and board officials.

Stern asked Raney to explain comments in his letter that were noted as condescending to the black culture. Though he had a valid point in his statement that the black colleges had not had access to the books, he was wrong in thinking that the students were not up to par, and his harsh criticism did not stop the fund from providing advanced-level literature to the black institutions. The fund refused Raney's offer to create a new list as Davis had initially informed the colleges that Curtis would be the point of information for book purchase and approvals as she held the leading role for collection development. Davis voiced, in a letter to Smith dated December 1927, that it would be disrespectful to Curtis if the fund allowed the University of Chicago professors to form a new graded-down list as she had worked diligently with the colleges. Curtis had also acquired competent assistance and counsel and for the past two to three years had visited and studied the library needs of black schools.[23]

Though Curtis was open to suggestions of additions and omissions, she was not willing to allow the current list to be a basis for a new list by those unfamiliar with the college and the students' needs and then publish it as a Hampton leaflet. The fund knew the Carnegie Corporation, which financed the Hampton library school, held her in high regard as did many librarians. The Hampton faculty selected the primary college library list, and faculty members of the University of Chicago provided assistance, but no one could deny the major contributions of Curtis, which led to the success of the college libraries. Officials knew that no one else had more information about the conditions prevailing in the libraries of black schools, no one else had given the matter more constructive thought, and no one else was in the position to be more continuously helpful in the future. Thus, her wishes were upheld by the fund. To the pleasure of many, including Curtis, Rosenwald had a change of heart and decided to allow his name to be used in connection with the aid given to black college libraries.

HIGH SCHOOL LIBRARIES

Unlike the experimental aid given to elementary rural schools and black colleges, the fund gave aid to high school libraries with further restrictions. These restrictions were a means to influence practices beyond the library. The archival documents record the commitment of the officials to developing high schools without limit. In 1926, the fund agreed to increase the size of the school buildings to nine- and ten-teacher type schools under the condition that the additional three or four rooms would be restricted to high school grade levels and a library. After implementation of these policies, a survey revealed that more than three-fourths of four-year high schools for blacks were housed in the larger Rosenwald schools.[24] The additional facilities enabled the state department of education to accelerate developing the modern high schools for blacks to state-approved levels and gain accreditation by the Southern Association of Colleges and Secondary Schools.

With policy-making organizations supporting developing African American high schools, the executive committee of the fund appropriated $20,000 to provide libraries for these schools beginning during the 1929–1930 academic year. The fund used this opportunity to enhance the library practices to achieve levels approved by the state department of education. In efforts to accomplish this goal, the fund officials agreed on four key points: (1) Offers were initially restricted to four-year high schools; (2) an inclusive list of books was created and approved by accrediting agencies of several states; (3) from the inclusive list, a smaller list was compiled to meet the requirements of the accrediting agencies of several states from which book sets could be assembled; and (4) aid was offered toward extending existing libraries in African American high schools where facilities were inadequate.[25] Purchase of the high school book sets was left to the state department of education with the understanding that the fund would pay one-third of the total cost and shipping charges.

The archival materials revealed many similarities between the elementary school and high school libraries, including responsibility for the book collections and a required course on caring for and using the library. It was evident that reading was greatly encouraged and proved beneficial. Still, officials approached developing high school libraries differently, noting that they were attempting to help an age group where the majority of library users did not have the benefit of literature available at a young age.

When it came to the library practices at the high school level, school and fund officials focused on two key elements: the amount of quality literature and the library facility. The elementary library sets held up to 150 titles, whereas the high school library contained 2,000 titles and a minimum of 15 periodicals. The Southern office in Nashville carefully prepared the list of books under the editorial supervision of Jackson E. Towne, librarian of Peabody College and consultant in library service for the Julius Rosenwald Fund. The fund worked with previously compiled lists, including those from Southern high school libraries, Curtis, the Standard Catalog for High School Libraries, and the American Library Association's 500-book high school list. The collective effort to build a sufficient list covering multiple disciplines in order to appeal to a varied audience proved to be beneficial to encouraging reading. Teachers were able to assist students and community members with a variety of interests, which fueled their desire to read and pursue further educational opportunities. [26]

During developing the high school library, the fund placed more emphasis on the library facility. Creating an adequate facility actually became a standard practice. As explained in the Fisk University special collections, the complete library is achieved only when the space has acquired a friendly atmosphere and calming character, which motions to the passing student or tugs at the heartstrings of the student who must not be late to class. [27] Ultimately, the goal was for the library to become the living room, or soul, of the school.

The fund and school officials sought to achieve this environment through establishing facility guidelines. The archival collection discloses the intense detail that went into creating a welcoming environment that encouraged readers of all ages. With a vast supply of reading material available in the library, the officials focused on 10 factors that created a warm setting. These areas considered the location, entrances and exits, number and type of rooms, dimensions and seating capacity, walls, built-ins, floor, heating and plumbing, lighting, and necessary equipment, including furniture. Today, the same factors are considered when developing libraries and bookstore reading spaces. The library set no longer was simply about providing reading material but now was also about exposing the students to a variety of topics they could learn from and potentially become enticed to pursue as a field of study. The levels of growth in child-age literacy was well recorded and most pleasing to fund officials who subsequently wanted to share the library service with the community on the same level.

COUNTY LIBRARIES

The ALA initially suggested the fund enter in the field by providing county library service. However, it was decided to focus on elementary and college libraries as these schools also serviced the local communities. After the 1927 library conference at Hampton, the thought was to establish the collegiate libraries and have the institutions extend library service by truck to the Rosenwald schools and local counties. [28] It was assumed this could take the place of the needed county library service and would be the sole financial responsibility of the college. This feat would be financially impossible for a black college in 1927 without major contributions from outside agencies. Naturally, and in most philanthropic of spirits, the Julius Rosenwald Fund board of trustees decided to take on this monumental task during a spring meeting in 1929 as the organization had already begun assisting libraries as part of the rural school program. The initial school-building program gave officials a firsthand glimpse at the need for library service as well as the need for trained African American librarians. On account of these facts, the fund was enthused to aid Southern library development through county libraries.

The Julius Rosenwald Fund developed a five-year county library demonstration with the intent of developing proper service in the given counties and to work out the optimum scope and methods of library service on a county-wide basis. Officials were very selective in choosing the demonstration libraries. Each library was strategically located from the point of view of their influence on the entire region. Also, the library board was required to provide an adequate library program of 50¢ per capita of the city and county population.[29] Unfortunately, Florida, Georgia, and Oklahoma were ineligible, as none of the states had made provisions to appropriate funds for library service. A lack of prosperity hindered Virginia and Kentucky and rendered them ineligible. Aid was made available to 11 county libraries for books and service, which was defined to include salaries, general maintenance, and book trucks.

The library service provided by the demonstration county libraries can be described as educational, recreational, and cultural. Services rendered by the public libraries included pay collections, regular circulation of books, and a variety of special programs. There were provisions established for formal adult education programs, musical and drama organizations, exhibits, art galleries, and the circulation of images, slides, music scores, and phonograph records.[30] Other specialized services included books for the blind, lectures, and museum collections available in certain locations.

The S. L. Smith collection provides many examples of the services rendered in the demonstration libraries. Many of the demonstration libraries were able to build relationships and create collaborations with local museums and schools. For example, in the Chattanooga Public Library, which sponsored a lecture series involving prominent people covering a variety of topics, all facilities and programs were open to the general public. The speaker would often provide annotated bibliographies with a highlight of titles held by the local library. Chattanooga's system also developed a government documents department, which operated in close connection with that of the University of Tennessee. In addition, due to aid from the fund, many of the county libraries were able to provide mobile service.

Many of the libraries purchased book trucks and mobile stations to service rural schools, community centers, hospitals, Boy and Girl Scouts head-

Young African American readers enjoying the bookmobile of the Roland B. Hayes Colored Branch, Chattanooga Public Library. *Fisk University, John Hope and Aurelia E. Franklin Library, Special Collections, Julius Rosenwald Fund Archives, 1917–1948, box 558, folder 6.*

quarters, and transient bureaus. Another example is the Jefferson County Library (Texas) collaboration with the Gates Memorial Library of Port Arthur to supply an indefinite loan of 800 books. Gates Memorial agreed to place 350 books with the Lincoln Black School of Port Arthur.[31]

The libraries were well supplied with literature covering various topics, much like the college and high school libraries, and held a wide range of volumes from nearly 14,000 in Davidson County, Tennessee, to more than 230,000 in Shelby County, Tennessee. However, the Rosenwald archives exposed disparities in the book stock. Though the program called for equal services to be granted to all persons of the county, blacks were often provided a smaller supply of books. For example, Mecklenburg County, North Carolina, held more than 106,246 volumes, but only 10,540 were for blacks.[32]

Though the statistics make it evident that not one of the demonstration libraries possessed a satisfactory book collection for servicing blacks, many of the libraries reported increased interest in the services at the branches and potential for wider development. For example, the demonstration library of Louisiana reported far more visitors from various parts of the parishes who inquired about the potential to develop services in their own parish. Also, the two South Carolina demonstration libraries largely contributed to statewide interest in libraries.[33] The fund continued to push forward in efforts to garner

Young readers enjoying the bookmobile of the Greenville Public Library, which promotes free reading materials. *Fisk University, John Hope and Aurelia E. Franklin Library, Special Collections, Julius Rosenwald Fund Archives, 1917–1948, box 558, folder 6.*

better opportunities for blacks because the county library demonstration greatly benefited local users and neighboring counties. This is something fund officials enjoyed sharing, especially when one of the demonstration libraries achieved a new level of service.

In order that each of the 11 county libraries participating in the demonstration had a better knowledge of what the others were doing, the fund sponsored the Intercounty Library News Bulletin. In the bulletin, each librarian from demonstration libraries agreed to issue a quarterly report giving a general statement of the library service in their county. Each of these letters contained thrilling progress and stories about readers interested in library service and education. In the initial edition (February 1936), Elizabeth Tombs of the Walker County Library in Alabama reported the circulation had increased steadily each year from 44,214 in 1931 to 290,626 in 1935, and the numbers of books demonstrate this growth. In 1931, the number of books was 9,098, whereas in 1936 the library's collection had grown to 22,000 volumes. Although there were only 7,813 blacks in the county, the circulation increased from 4,853 in 1931 to 23,064 in 1935.[34] Special attention was given to the schools in the county due to the county board of education's $4,500 contribution to the annual appropriations. In 1934, a general reference collection was purchased for each of the seven accredited high schools of the county.

The Webster Parish Library of Louisiana reported the parish had lacked library service completely prior to establishing the parish system. As the income of the library had been less than 50¢ per capita, sometimes down to 43¢ some years, officials used their best judgment during operation. Upon establishment, the same library collection serviced the community, high school, and grammar school, all with one librarian or custodian (untrained) in charge. Though the parish school board provided a facility, equipment, and salary for the librarian, the collections and facility were inadequate. With the assistance of the Julius Rosenwald Fund, by 1936, there were 12 white library branches and 14 for blacks. The number of active library users was 14,732, which was nearly 50 percent of the population. Webster was considered to be a typical Southern county in that the population is almost entirely rural; there were small farmers with small incomes and a county government with a small income. The parish, as well as the other 10 demonstration libraries, had gone far to prove that the average small-town person would read if given the opportunity.

The collections also revealed much of the data that was included in a 1935 study of the county library demonstration conducted by Louis Wilson and Edward Wight of the Graduate Library School at the University of Chicago. The fund appropriated $7,500 for the study. The purpose of the study was (1) to describe the organization, development, and the operation of the libraries; (2) to evaluate their services; and (3) to compare the service near and outside the area.[35] The collections also hold the required data concerning registration, circulation, and the book collection for each library. This study would greatly assist in potential future research projects.

GEOGRAPHIC AREA

The fund's board of trustees decided to aid in library development based on known conditions concerning the South. The entire Southern region was definitely behind in library development. This was made apparent in a study revealing 71 percent of the population was without access to library facilities. This was mainly due to the low allotment per capita for public library service, which ranged from 18¢ in Florida down to 2¢ in Mississippi. This was far below the national average of 33¢ per capita. In addition, the region could not afford to provide adequate library services due to its low fiscal status compared to other regions. It was a large rural, segregated area that would need to provide a facility for each of two races. Very few areas in the South provided services to blacks. Prior to 1929, neither county nor state government had made attempts to provide satisfactory library service to rural blacks that were comparable to the efforts that built the rural schools or promoted public health.[36] Consequently, the service for both groups, black and white, was undeveloped.

TIME PERIOD

The library program officially began contributing to developing Southern libraries in 1927 starting with 10 libraries in each participating Southern state and five teacher training colleges. As time progressed, more rural libraries joined those with the notable Rosenwald-funded stamp of approval as now able to provide books and a variety of services. Fund officials witnessed success in the various divisions of the library program and gradually extended the services as money allowed. Many of these libraries were funded when aid was plentiful. However, most found difficulty in maintaining satisfactory appropriations and services during the depression years of the early 1930s. Yet, because of the heroic efforts of the librarians and determined community members, the libraries managed to keep the services going at reasonably adequate levels. Beyond the funding, the people involved in the library program (fund officials, librarians, consultants, and community members) were instrumental to the consistent success of the program during its nearly 10-year operation.

From 1927 until March 1941, the fund distributed 9,402 libraries (7,191 for elementary schools and 2,211 for high schools). From July 1928 until June 1934, the fund appropriated monies for the acquisition and development of book collections in 43 black colleges and normal schools. From 1929 until 1936, 11 county libraries participated in the demonstration with the initial five years of funding provided by the Julius Rosenwald Fund Library Program, which led to the organization helping a number of other libraries and organizations. Though no evidence presented itself in the archival documents that stated there was a set time period to operate the library program, the fund achieved its goal to provide literature in efforts to enhance the reading abilities and educational opportunities to African Americans in the rural South in an optimal time frame.

EMERGENT CODES

During data collection, I remained open so that codes not previously considered could emerge freely. Information on the fund's move to aid library development by providing funding to various agencies of influence repeatedly appeared. Officials believed the selected agencies would benefit the geographic area on a larger scale than the county library demonstration. Upon further analysis, I determined there was enough information in the archival documents to identify each area as an emergent code. This section of the chapter examines emergent contributions to state library commissions, library schools, scholarships and fellowships, institutes and meetings, and extended library service, and library sets for servicemen.

STATE LIBRARY COMMISSIONS

Administrators for the library program recognized that the most effective agency in establishing new library systems and improving existing service in any state was a properly organized and adequately supported state library commission. The fund provided aid for developing state library commissions in the hope that the external aid would encourage the state to contribute in efforts to increase the effectiveness of library commissions previously created. The board of trustees agreed to grant monies to state library commissions in four Southern states where the Rosenwald library program was already operative. Combined, the fund provided $21,000 to the state library commissions of Alabama, Arkansas, South Carolina, and Tennessee.

Arkansas and Tennessee were assisted in increasing the state budget to provide an allotment for a library commission on a dollar-to-dollar basis for two years. While a similar offer was made to Mississippi, the state was unable to meet the fund's requirements. Though Alabama and South Carolina had previously established state library commissions, they had no paid staff prior to the fund's involvement. Both states were assisted in establishing provisions of the budget to include a state library field-worker on a three-year basis. The aid was granted with the understanding that when the three-year period came to an end, the state would be financially responsible for the service of the field worker.[37] In addition, the fund covered the traveling expenses for the field-workers of seven Southern states to attend various conferences and workshops focused on library extension programs in rural areas. Without aid, the additional training would not have been possible for most of the field-workers. The progressive work with developing libraries in the South through state library commissions contributed to fulfilling the desires for library services and led to region-wide stimulation.

LIBRARY SCHOOLS

One of the conditions made by the fund when granting aid to the county libraries was that the county employed a trained librarian. However, the county library was not always able to do so. One reason was the deficiency in the number of trained librarians. It was suggested by the ALA that the fund include in its library program a policy of aiding the establishment of library schools. The officers regarded the project of training librarians as having a crucial bearing on the success of the entire library program in the South. The fund made financial contributions to two influential library schools, Hampton Institute and Emory University.

The Hampton Institute Library Science School was established in September 1925 by a grant from the Carnegie Corporation for educating African American librarians. The founding was fully endorsed by the Julius Rosenwald Fund, which made appropriations of $16,000 for Curtis's travel expenses and compensation for her visits to various black colleges to assess the library status and needs as well as stimulate the college's interest in developing modern library services and facilities. The appropriations also paid for the salary of an assistant director.[38] At the time of the establishment of Hampton's library school, the Carnegie Library School of Atlanta (1905–1925) was the only accredited library school in the South; however, it trained only white librarians.

The experience of Rosenwald and the fund in making contributions to the libraries of black colleges and normal schools in the South made clear the need for the advice and counsel of trained librarians. Thus, the fund sought to further contribute to the production of properly educated librarians. On November 20, 1929, the fund appropriated $50,000 on a five-year period ending August 31, 1935, to Emory University for the establishment and maintenance of the Atlanta Library School (formerly the Carnegie Library School) as a department of the university. This appropriation was made on the condition that $20,000 would be obtained for the same purpose from other sources.[39] The Atlanta Library School operated from 1930 until 1988 on the campus of Emory University.

SCHOLARSHIPS AND FELLOWSHIPS

The fund also contributed numerous scholarships to induce promising black men and women to take on work in the library field. Sixteen scholarships were granted to the Hampton Institute Library School for students from important Southern college, city, and county libraries. Upon graduation, the newly trained librarians returned to service. The Atlanta Library School at Emory University was the recipient of nine scholarships at $1,000 each, between 1930 and 1931, which enticed promising young men. The archival documents listed an additional gift in 1942 of $4,000 for scholarships to train county library coordinators.[40]

Though fellowships directly to individuals was not a part of the fund's library program, it is appropriate to note that between 1929 and 1934, the fund granted 34 scholarships totaling $32,100 to black women and men pursing administrative roles in libraries.[41] Library administration ranked fourth in the number of scholarships awarded out of a total of 20 subjects.

The majority of the recipients studied at Hampton. The fellowships helped to elevate the training of notable librarians, including Vivian G. Harsh, who became Chicago Public Library System's first black librarian with a branch named for her contributions, and Dorothy Porter-Wesley, who played a primary role in building Howard University's collection and with materials for the study of black history and culture.

INSTITUTES AND MEETINGS

Funds were also given for summer institutes and meetings of Southern librarians totaling $1,827. Some of the benefactors include 1929 summer institutes for teacher-librarians in Virginia and North Carolina, a conference for the policy committee of the Southeastern Library Association, and small sums for the attendance of select Southern librarians at the National Institute for Library Field Agents in Wisconsin.[42] In November 1929, the fund allocated $10,000 for conducting a summer institute for black librarians at Atlanta University. The program was active July and August 1930 and successfully hosted 35 librarians. However, the institute only required $3,381, allowing for the balance to lapse. Lastly, the fund appropriated one-third of the costs of the "Conference of Negro Librarians" held November 20–23, 1930, at Fisk University under the direction of head librarian Louis Shores.[43]

EXTENDED LIBRARY SERVICE TO AFRICAN AMERICAN CITIES

The Julius Rosenwald Fund provided extended library service to museums and libraries in cities with a high African American population. In connection with the county library demonstration, the fund appropriated $7,000 for the Charleston Museum of South Carolina in 1929, with funding based on the condition that $5,000 would be used for continued educational extension work and the balance for the director's travel expenses and other activities.[44] This appropriation was made to enlarge the exceptional work of the museum in extension education with a focus on the traveling exhibits to black and white rural schools. With this collaboration proving to be beneficial to the students, the fund decided to extend library service to predominately African American county and city libraries.

In 1931, Mobile Public Library (Alabama) and Richmond Public Library (Virginia) were each appropriated $2,500 to develop a library branch for African Americans. They were required to use the funding for a trained librarian and an adequate book supply. While $1,795 was spent during 1931–1933, the balance was allowed to lapse because the library system was unable to maintain the branch at the level stipulated by the fund. Further north, Richmond was granted funding on a three-year period ending December 31, 1934. For every $1 paid by the fund, Richmond was required to match with $2. Like the Mobile Library System, funds were to be used for the salary of a trained black librarian and books. Of the sum, $910 was appropriated for the salary and $372 for the book supply. However, this turned out to be a mirror image of the Mobile system as the Richmond Public Library System was unable to meet the conditions set forth at the time of appropriation, causing the balance to lapse.[45]

The fund also extended library service to two large cities with a predominately black population. During June 1931, $15,000 was granted for a three-year experiment for an extension program focused on library service and adult education at the Auburn branch in Atlanta, Georgia, and at the 135th Street branch in Harlem, New York. The appropriation was made on the condition that $30,000 would be raised from other sources. The additional funding would soon come from the Carnegie Corporation at the rate of $10,000 per year, meeting the fund's condition. Atlanta was granted $6,000 per year, while Harlem was granted $9,000 per year. The Atlanta branch spent $3,000 for an adequate book supply and $9,000 for salaries. The Harlem branch spent $14,000 for salaries and $3,000 for lectures. Each branch spent the balance on operations, travel, and other miscellaneous expenses.[46] Both libraries have been a staple in public library history, from the establishment of each through the Harlem Renaissance and the civil rights movement.

LIBRARIES FOR MILITARY SERVICEMEN

The fund created and distributed five libraries (book sets) for black and white rural schools in Southern states. The libraries included books that were comprehensive in style, interesting in subject matter, and appealing in format. The sets were made available to thousands of rural schools at two-thirds the cost with the fund absorbing the remaining third as well as freight charges.[47] Though the sets were created to enrich a culture and a region, the organization still sought to make a boarder impact. The fund looked at the nation's treatment of blacks and sought to influence that outlook as well. The war presented the perfect opportunity to do so.

During World War II, many men left the comfort of their homes and lived closely with a group of men of varying national origin, religion, and background for the time. The change in living quarters often led to an increased understanding of persons and groups previously considered different or inferior. In contrast, some biases were so strong that feelings remained unchanged. It was felt that accurate information concerning the different groups that made up America would serve to extend further the servicemen's understanding of all his fellow citizens. Subsequently, the fund assembled a selection of books and pamphlets on race relations, which was offered free to any active army or navy posts and general hospitals in the country that requested them. The offer was later extended to the Veteran Administration hospitals, making the Race Relations Library available to thousands of servicemen during the war.

Archival documents reveal an agency created by a man who was determined to assist in diminishing the plight of African Americans through efforts that would increase literacy levels and educational opportunities. Library practices began with small library sets and soon increased to large library sets holding 2,000 titles and 15 periodicals and led to libraries facilitating themselves. With this grand level of dedication and financial assistance, the library became the heart of each school, freely circulating and woven into the curriculum of various subjects. In addition, the libraries were established to enlighten those rural counties and states not funded by Rosenwald of the benefits of library service. Subsequently, the influence spread throughout the Southern region. Desire for an increase in literature and services occurred in neighboring libraries of schools and universities. Growth in the available books, services, and trained librarians was Rosenwald's goal, and it was well achieved, providing a forever impact on the lives of African American users and the Southern region.

NOTES

1. Fisk University, Special Collections and Archives, S. L. Smith Collection, box 11, folder 10.

2. S. L. Smith, "Library Facilities in Negro Secondary Schools," *Journal of Negro Education* 9, no. 3 (1940): 504–12.

3. J. Noland, "Jeanes Supervisors," in *Encyclopedia of Alabama*, July 2, 2009, para. 4, http://www.encyclopediaofalabama.org/article/h-2327.

4. Fisk University, Special Collections and Archives, Samuel Leonard Smith Collection, box 11, folder 10.

5. Fisk University, John and Aurelia E. Franklin Library, Special Collections, S. L. Smith Collection, box 42, folder 5.

6. Smith, "Library Facilities."

7. Ibid.

8. Ibid., 507–12.

9. Fisk University, Special Collections and Archives, S. L. Smith Collection, box 11, folder 10.

10. Fisk University, John Hope and Aurelia E. Franklin Library, Special Collections, S. L. Smith Collection, box 8, folder 7.

11. Fisk University, John and Aurelia E. Franklin Library, Special Collections, Julius Rosenwald Fund Archives, box 129, folder 1.

12. Fisk University, John and Aurelia E. Franklin Library, Special Collections, S. L. Smith Collection, box 42, folder 5.

13. Fisk University, John and Aurelia E. Franklin Library, Special Collections, Julius Rosenwald Fund Archives, box 262, folder 1.

14. Ibid.

15. Ibid.

16. Fisk University, John and Aurelia E. Franklin Library, Special Collections, S. L. Smith Collection, box 42, folder 5.

17. S. L. Smith, "The Julius Rosenwald Library Program," *American School Board Journal* (November 1948).
18. Fisk University, John and Aurelia E. Franklin Library, Special Collections, S. L. Smith Collection, box 42, folder 5.
19. Fisk University, John and Aurelia E. Franklin Library, Special Collections, Julius Rosenwald Fund Archives, box 262, folder 1.
20. Fisk University, John and Aurelia E. Franklin Library, Special Collections, S. L. Smith Collection, box 42, folder 5.
21. Ibid.
22. Ibid.
23. Fisk University, John and Aurelia E. Franklin Library, Special Collections, Julius Rosenwald Fund Archives, box 261, folder 5.
24. Smith, "Library Facilities," 507–12.
25. Fisk University, John and Aurelia E. Franklin Library, Special Collections, Julius Rosenwald Fund Archives, box 281, folder 2.
26. Fisk University, John and Aurelia E. Franklin Library, Special Collections, S. L. Smith Collection, box 8, folder 4.
27. Fisk University, John and Aurelia E. Franklin Library, Special Collections, S. L. Smith Collection, box 56, folder 13.
28. Fisk University, John and Aurelia E. Franklin Library, Special Collections, Julius Rosenwald Fund Archives, box 261, folder 5.
29. Fisk University, John and Aurelia E. Franklin Library, Special Collections, Julius Rosenwald Fund Archives, box 259, folder 15.
30. Fisk University, John and Aurelia E. Franklin Library, Special Collections, S. L. Smith Collection, box 8, folder 8.
31. Ibid.
32. Fisk University, John and Aurelia E. Franklin Library, Special Collections, S. L. Smith Collection, box 9, folder 6.
33. Fisk University, John and Aurelia E. Franklin Library, Special Collections, S. L. Smith Collection, box 11, folder 10.
34. Fisk University, John and Aurelia E. Franklin Library, Special Collections, S. L. Smith Collection, box 8, folder 8.
35. Fisk University, John and Aurelia E. Franklin Library, Special Collections, Julius Rosenwald Fund Archives, box 266, folder 2.
36. Fisk University, John and Aurelia E. Franklin Library, Special Collections, Julius Rosenwald Fund Archives, box 76, folder 12.
37. Ibid.
38. Fisk University, John and Aurelia E. Franklin Library, Special Collections, Julius Rosenwald Fund Archives, box 129, folder 5.
39. Fisk University, John and Aurelia E. Franklin Library, Special Collections, Julius Rosenwald Fund Archives, box 258, folder 9.
40. Fisk University, John and Aurelia E. Franklin Library, Special Collections, Julius Rosenwald Fund Archives, box 258, folder 3.
41. Ibid.
42. Fisk University, John and Aurelia E. Franklin Library, Special Collections, S. L. Smith Collection, box 8, folder 7.
43. Fisk University, John and Aurelia E. Franklin Library, Special Collections, S. L. Smith, box 8, folder 8.
44. Ibid.
45. Ibid.
46. Fisk University, John and Aurelia E. Franklin Library, Special Collections, Julius Rosenwald Fund Archives, box 260, folder 1.
47. Fisk University, John and Aurelia E. Franklin Library, Special Collections, Julius Rosenwald Fund Archives, box 260, folder 9.

Chapter Four

Standardizing Black Librarianship

The American Library Association (ALA) reported that, in 1948, 45 million people in the United States lived in areas unable to offer library services due to lack of development, including infrastructure, funding, and access regulations.[1] With the exception of larger cities, the majority of African Americans lacked service. For those cities that were fortunate enough to offer service to blacks, there were a number of inadequacies concerning the facility, book collection, and personnel. These matters were already popular topics of conversation within the library community, specifically among African American library workers. As a result of such conversations that predated the ALA's report, a library conference at Hampton Institute (founded 1925) was organized enlisting the participation of a variety of library workers. From various discussions, participants focused on the lack of reading materials, adequate facilities, professional development, and funding needed to provide all things for suitable library service to students as well as the community. The 1927 Hampton Library Conference was a conscious step toward improving library services for African Americans. The conference also raised major concerns regarding the formal education and professional training of African American librarians.

Black librarianship, like a variety of Negro professions, institutions, and organizations, was delayed by the Jim Crow way of life, accreditation, and a lack of funding. Melville Dewey (1851–1931) established the first American school of librarianship, formerly called the School of Library Economy of Columbia College (now Columbia University), in 1887 with a class of 20 students.[2] However, African Americans would not gain formal education in the area until 1900 when Edward Christopher Williams (1871–1929) became the first African American librarian to receive a library degree from the New York State Library School (Albany). He continued his formal education until his sudden passing in 1929.[3] Twenty-three years later, Virginia Proctor Powell Florence (1897–1991) became the first African American woman, and only the second African American, formally educated in library science when she graduated from the Carnegie Library School (Pittsburgh) in 1923.[4] By 1925, there were six formally educated African American librarians.[5]

Opening the library school at Hampton Institute (1925–1939) documented a level of persistent demand in the maturity of a culture's literacy and the need to uplift itself. Prior to the conceptual development and establishment of the library school at Hampton Institute, there were educational opportunities in the form of training programs for African Americans interested in library work. During the early twentieth century, 1910 to circa 1931, the notable Louisville Free Public Library created (out of necessity for black library assistants) an apprenticeship program, which trained 42 people for library work.[6] Though a great initiative, the program made it evident that training on a larger scale, a degree-granting program, for African Americans was long overdue. The next step in creating such a program was crucial, not only for diversity within the field but also for granting library services in black communities as well as advocacy for higher-level educational opportunities. Figa and Macpherson cite Dumont's 1986 report that detailed three key reasons for Hampton being selected as the location for the inaugural library science program, specifically designed to train African American librarians, over Fisk, Howard, and Tuskegee. Those reasons: (1) Hampton, at the time, held a significant book collection in a standing library in good condition with trained staff; (2) the institute allowed hiring multiracial faculty, which meant they could hire qualified white faculty to teach (assisted in leveling the field with knowledge granted at other, predominantly white institutions [PWI]); and (3) the institute's black alumni held leadership positions throughout the South, equipping the program with adequate ability to assist in the placement of the library school's graduates.[7] There is also the argument that Hampton was selected based on the influence of whites in power who felt it was important to maintain the status quo of decision-making authority for blacks, even in library science education. These leaders likely did not have the same level of influence at Fisk, Howard, and Tuskegee.

Hampton Institute's library school was established with financial support from the Julius Rosenwald Fund, the General Education Board, and the Carnegie Corporation. The opening was important not only for developing African American librarianship but also for the library science field. In 1925, the only other accredited Southern library science program was Emory University's Library School (Atlanta), formerly the Carnegie Library School of Atlanta (1905–1925). However, the Southern library school did not desegregate until 1962, accepting its first class of African American students in the fall of 1963.[8] In addition, the library became a focal point for state and regional accrediting agencies as they began to better understand the influence the resources had on the school's educational programs. Hampton was able to counter discrimination and assist in accrediting many black colleges by emphasizing its placement program. The library school limited annual enrollment to 15 to 20 black students due to the limited number of positions available in the region for African Americans. A calculated decision as a major consideration for a school's success rate is directly related to the number of graduates working in the degreed field. In total, Hampton graduated 183 black librarians.[9]

A major influence on the success of Hampton's program as well as its involvement with the Rosenwald Fund Library Program was the first director of Hampton's library school, Florence Rising Curtis. She was a well-respected champion for black librarianship who happened to be a white woman. She was a graduate of the New York State Library School (1898) and held positions as a professor at the University of Illinois and vice director at Drexel Institute (Philadelphia), where she assisted in establishing the undergraduate library science program.[10] Selflessly, Curtis traveled throughout the South, discussing the needs and interests at black colleges with the presidents and faculty. Her travels, initially funded by the Rosenwald Fund, resulted in the vast development of library facilities and services by providing assistance with everything from book selection to building design, along with regular communication, personnel training, and advising reader services.[11] During the first Negro Library Conference held in Hampton (1927), Curtis highlighted the need for gradual development due to the lack of trained librarians. She also emphasized a need for those servicing patrons to have some form of academic training, though college graduation was preferable. Successful primary teachers were thought to make great librarians and were continuously recommended to the Hampton Institute Library School.

JULIUS ROSENWALD AND HISTORICALLY BLACK COLLEGES AND UNIVERSITIES LIBRARIES

The initial concept for the library program focused on the rural Rosenwald schools as many were already operating with multiple generations in one location but were void of proper reading materials. Simultaneously, the need for materials at black colleges was viewed as equally crucial. A number of black colleges began as normal schools, also known as teacher training colleges. Yet they lacked teaching materials including children's literature. In addition, this lack of literature also meant that the college students were unable to learn appropriate use and care for books and, in some cases, healthy reading habits to share with school-aged children. In essence, any teacher training program without an ample amount of reading materials and children's literature lacked standardization, and the possibility of closing was a real consideration. With the minimum opportunity for blacks to attend college and the few historically black colleges and universities to select from, due to race relations, the prospect of closure had to be prevented. Literacy was the blanket solution to the teacher training colleges, normal schools, rural schools, and ultimately the growth of the African American culture. These facts may have been a catalyst for field agent of the General Education Board Jackson Davis's desire to increase access to African Americans starting with schoolbooks and going on to children's literature.

Historically black colleges and universities (HBCUs) were established as a means to support the educational demands of African Americans while also preserving a cultural history. However, the schools often lacked the appropriate funding to maintain all aspects of higher learning, including educational offerings. The lack of suitable resources delayed, and in some cases prevented, accreditation.[12] Due to racism and the segregation of public black colleges, these institutions were starved for proper facilities, qualified faculty, salaries, and overall support, which was easily accessible at PWIs. A number of HBCUs were established with a church or religious affiliation, making them ineligible for state funding due to the First Amendment, specifically the concept of separation between church and state.[13] This command prohibited the use of taxpayer money to fund religious organizations or those with a church affiliation, despite Southern state departments of education's refusal to support black schools and colleges. In essence, they were set up to fail. Many HBCU libraries lacked a trained librarian, an adequate building, modern equipment and furniture, and a collection of usable books to accommodate the readers. This was a rightful concern as most institutional libraries also serviced the local African American community.

In efforts to enhance library services, philanthropist Julius Rosenwald assisted in establishing the Hampton Institute's Library Science School for training African American librarians. Soon after, he agreed to grant experimental aid to five Negro teacher training colleges, none of which possessed an adequate library or trained personnel. As previously mentioned, the inaugural five colleges selected were Tennessee Agricultural and Industrial State College, Southern University, Tuskegee Institute, Petersburg Normal and Industrial Institute, and North Carolina College. Five became six when Winston-Salem Teachers College was added because it specialized in upper-level teacher training for elementary schools, while the other institutions trained teachers for all grade levels.[14] The administration, financial planning, and stipulations for the HBCU libraries were detailed in the previous chapter. Naturally, minds wondered about the state of the experimental colleges at the closure of the fund.

The 1948 ALA review revealed that each library had become the heart of the institution, imperative to every department. As a result of the funding provided by the Julius Rosenwald Fund, a number of significant changes took place, including: (1) the value of the facility, equipment and furniture, and books increased from $20,000 to $2.5 million; (2) number of volumes went from 300,000 to 6,000 suitable volumes in 1927–1928; (3) overall library budget for books, periodicals, and trained library service increased from $6,000 to $225,000; and (4) the number of full-time librarians was 48 in 1948 compared to 6 part-time untrained librarians in 1927–1928. Then there are the monumental changes that are bigger than numbers, such as each college receiving accreditation by state and regional agencies. In addition, each of the participating colleges was able to boast a number of professors including presidents who held doctorate degrees from top universities in the country, unlike during the 1927–1928 school year when no institution could make such a highlight on their application.[15] With an experiment, individual results varied, and the library program was no exception. Fortunately, this trial benefited all involved.

Agricultural and Industrial State College (Tennessee State University) was the only state-supported Negro college in Tennessee, making it simple for them to qualify with agreement to financial requirements and planning the erection of a $100,000 fireproof library in the heart of the campus. They immediately selected an exemplary instructor and sent her to the Hampton Institution Library Science School on a General Education Board scholarship. The initial library operated with one classroom with a few books and a part-time librarian but soon grew to a modern library with 35,000 volumes, 450 up-to-date magazines and journals, and 20,000 government documents from the U.S. Department of Agriculture, the Office of Education, and other federal agencies. Archival documents acknowledge more than 80,000 items circulated during the 1947–1948 school year, in addition to the use of multiple reading rooms.

The staff increased to 10 full-time librarians, four of whom held a bachelor of science in library science, one with a master of science in library science, and others with professional training. The operating budget increased 50 times and the state's board of education provided $700,000 for an addition to the building and facility. The large facilities housed 120,000 volumes, plenty of reading room space for more than 2,000 students, and other spaces that deemed the facility one of the most modern libraries in the state of Tennessee in 1948. The approval as a four-year college and graduate school by the state's board of education, the Southern Association of Colleges, and the American Association of Colleges for Teacher Education has been credited to the new library facilities.

Southern University's library program opened with a few books and a small reading room. In order to qualify for the offer from the Rosenwald Fund, the university accepted the terms, remodeled and equipped the auditorium with library furniture, and selected an outstanding teacher to send to

Hampton. The new library opened with $3,000 worth of new books selected from a preapproved list by Hampton and continued to grow with an annual budget of $3,000 for books until 1941 when a fireproof library building was built. The total cost was $125,000, not including an additional $10,000 for library equipment. As a result of the numerous improvements, the annual book budget range grew to $9,000–11,000. With such a generous account, the library acquired 38,812 volumes and 250 periodicals that supplemented the curriculum for student circulation of nearly 200,000. The library employed seven full-time staff members including five who earned a library science degree, one paraprofessional, and a clerk. In addition, the library also employed several part-time student workers.

In a turn of events, Southern University's library established a film and audio archive. Serving as a regional film depository of the state for elementary and high schools, colleges, and hospitals, the library held 679 recordings and transcriptions used for teaching purposes. Such improvements, including the new library facility and renewed relationship with the state as a regional depository, played a major role in helping the college to qualify for approval by the Southern Association of Colleges.

Tuskegee Institute (Tuskegee University), like the other participant institutions, long felt the need to develop a library with children's literature. Naturally, they accepted the offer's conditions, improved their library facilities, and selected an exemplary teacher to go to Hampton. The university was able to build a modern library through gifts from friends of the library who were inspired by the fund's mission. The library facility cost a quarter million dollars, allowing the library to grow from a small collection of books and magazines to more than 80,000 volumes, more than 700 magazines and journals, and annual additions of 6,000 volumes, not counting thousands of state and federal publications. At the close of the fund, the library staff consisted of 13 members. The majority was professionally trained in library services; five held a bachelor of science in library science, and two earned a master of science in library science. Initially the university was not accredited, but it evolved into a renowned four-year college with graduate work approved by state and regional accrediting agencies. The library played a major role in instructional programming and securing an annual appropriation from the state of Alabama.

Petersburg Normal and Industrial Institute (Virginia State College) followed suit for qualifications to receive the library program offer. Following the initial gift, the fund granted an additional $100,000 toward the $400,000 building project. The General Education Board also provided additional grants toward the program, which stimulated increased support from the state. With the abundance of financial support, the college built a library facility at the cost of $171,050 with modern furniture and equipment. The new facility held a total of 40,506 volumes and 307 periodicals selected to meet the needs of the undergraduate and graduate curriculum. The library staff was no exception to the program's growth, increasing to five full-time professionally trained librarians, one clerk, and a grand total of 20 student workers. By 1948, the library budget for books, services, and operating expenses had grown to more than $44,000.

North Carolina College (North Carolina Central University), according to the state auditor in 1927, was valued at a little over $700, including the physical plant, equipment, and books. The college quickly qualified for the full grant amount of $2,500 from Rosenwald. A teacher was selected to go to Hampton library school, and no argument was made against the stipulations. Initially, administrators were limited to relocating the library to a double classroom in the administration building. This changed with a rapid increase in interest and an attractive proposal for the liberal arts college and graduate school, resulting in a new library facility (1935). Also, the general assembly appropriated $550,000 for a library to accommodate 800 readers and 200,000 volumes and to house the library school. The large library provided spaces for other graduate divisions. The new library's personnel consisted of eight full-time staff members of which three held a bachelor of science in library science and four earned a master of science in library science. In addition to the staff members who were formally educated, one staff member held a law degree. At the time of review, the library held a total of 53,088 volumes waiting to be cataloged. Once the new library was built, the original was converted into a law library with staff and 45,000 volumes, enabling the school to maintain a high level of efficiency.

Winston-Salem Teachers College (Winston-Salem State University) started with a library space consisting of two uneven-sized rooms in a classroom building with a few books and a part-time librarian. Upon qualifying for funding and accepting terms, a modern library was built in the administration building with a $105,000 price tag in addition to $15,000 for furniture. The building was rightfully erected in the center of the campus with spacious and well-equipped reading rooms. The plan made provisions for book and art exhibits. The library was also equipped with specialized reading rooms, including those for browsing, children's literature, and reference books that each increased the effectiveness of the library facility.

With several floors, the library built in special book elevators to transport the more than 25,000 volumes and 243 magazines. In order to properly train teachers for higher grade levels in elementary schools, the college focused its literary selections on children's literature. The new library was operated by four trained librarians with library science degrees and 30 part-time student assistants on an annual operating budget of more than $16,000. This growth inspired the involvement of other philanthropists looking to assist in the intellectual enrichment, as well as honor late family members. One major contributor was William A. Whitaker, vice chairman of the college board of trustees, who made a substantial gift to purchase children's books and establish the Whitaker Memorial Children's Room in memory of his father. With the number of improvements, unique features, and services, the college was granted accreditation in February 1948 by the American Association of Colleges for Teacher Education, which noted, "The library is one of the outstanding features of the college, both in its housing and service to faculty and students. The library staff had a very high degree of professional spirit and rendering service to the college."[16]

EXTENDS FINANCIAL SUPPORT FOR HBCU LIBRARIES

Like the rural school experiment, once proven successful to the communities serviced, the Julius Rosenwald Fund continued its task to uplift a culture through literacy, and the fund expanded the library program's college division. Though the initial intention was to help the experimental five colleges and later assist a few other libraries in securing trucks and increased book collections for a library extension service to Rosenwald schools and other facilities in their respective districts or counties, the program rapidly expanded to include more than 40 HBCU libraries over a five-year period. Similar stipulations and a library plan were offered with a decrease in funding to help as many as possible. The initial six were granted $1 for every $2 raised (up to $2,500), whereas the extension also offered $1 for every $3 raised for books. Each college was granted the foundation for a modern library and trained librarians ready to accommodate the needs of the college. Records from the S. L. Smith collection and the Julius Rosenwald Fund archives offer evidence concerning the approval for accreditation of all the colleges by state and regional agencies as a result of the library program's generous aid and what the colleges where able to accomplish with the funding.

Between 1927 and 1930, Rosenwald granted $60,600 in library aid and $182,800 for the purchase of books in African American colleges and state schools (see the end of this chapter). The colleges were divided among 16 states, mostly along the East Coast, in the southeast region of the country. An administrator (often the president) or trained librarian was sent general report forms to complete that would demonstrate the funded-library's development over the course of participation or the full five years. The report form requested estimates on funding spent on librarian and staff salaries, the facility, and books, as well as volumes added to the overall collection. The figure on the next page documents how a few of the colleges were able to grow their libraries.[17]

Prior to funding, little to no money was available for library improvements at these historically black colleges and universities. Many library ad-

Institution	Funding Spent on the Facility	Books	Volumes Added	Total Expenditures for Salaries
A & M College (Arkansas)	$20,000.00	$7,500.00	4,402	$10,100.00
Florida A&M College (Florida)	$5,400.00	$10,000.00	5,835	$10,642.50
Livingstone College	$2,500.00	$3,500.00	3,710	$7,020.00
State N&I Institute (Prairie View, TX)	$1,538.33	$11,446.30	3,052	$17,118.60

College library development funded by the library program, 1932 report.

ministrators, such as J. B. Watson, president of A&M College in Pine Bluff, Arkansas, mentioned that the form did not take into account the number of staff members sent to library training workshops, which the fund also supported. State N&I Institute of Prairie View, Texas, reported they were unable to secure an entire building but moved into the new education building where the third floor housed the library and its operations, and two trained librarians were employed due to the financial assistance of the fund. In other institutions, administrators had the ability to hire and secure trained librarians, but in those cases there were no librarians at the facility.

In a lengthy, five-year report submitted to Smith by Mary McLeod Bethune, president of Bethune-Cookman College (now Bethune-Cookman University in Daytona Beach, Florida), dated April 28, 1932, Bethune noted the institution was finally able to secure a trained librarian in 1930 thanks to the funding. Through the financial assistance given by the fund and the General Education Board, Bethune-Cookman was able to add book worth $4,500. The library was open to the community as it was the only library for blacks in the area.[18] With more patronage, improved facilities, and the availability of a variety of literature, circulation increased beyond expectations, and concerns were raised. Worries included preservation needs like binding magazines and other periodicals for in-house use only, retiring damaged items, and ordering multiples of the same book or volume. Problems caused by constant circulation, which was welcomed, also required additional funding.[19]

The college boasted a number of services to the school, city, county, and state as well as accomplishments like establishing a teacher reserve book collection, the Detroit self-charging system and a borrower's register, and accession records books. The librarian built relationships with local churches and the community in order to address the value of the library (embedded librarianship and public space); created programs that dramatized books highlighting the accomplishments of prominent blacks and hosted programs from other departments; surveyed college libraries in the state; and attended the Negro Library Conference at Fisk University.

One could argue that recruitment efforts also improved as a result of the library funding because the new and improved facilities were a selling point for accrediting agencies, which gave the black colleges something to boast about, especially in the South. The president of Stowe College (now Harris-Stowe State University in St. Louis, Missouri) reported the major improvements to the library received "high commendations" from the American Association of Colleges for Teacher Education and the North Carolina Central Association of Colleges and Secondary Schools. In another case, Bethune-Cookman revealed how they endured a 28-year struggle trying to build a sufficient library as they only had the financial ability to do a little each year. In 1927, the college began to focus on its standardization where the library was a key component. While they diligently raised money for the college library, the fund offered aid (1929), which allowed aggressive advances including securing a trained librarian.

The growth continued, and as soon as some college libraries expanded, they were met with an increase in needs. For example, James Shepard, president of North Carolina College for Negroes, highlighted in his 1932 report that "our present facilities are totally inadequate for the growing student body," though the present facility would not have been possible without the aid from the Rosenwald Fund. Thus, plans were constantly being made for additional space and volumes to be added by the thousands to effectively serve the student body and faculty. Some even had to expand their hours, like Tougaloo College that reported the need to evolve from operating only during school hours to every Saturday 8:00 a.m. to midnight, and every other weekday 8:00 a.m. to midnight, 1:30 p.m. to 5:00 p.m., and 7:00 p.m. to 9 p.m.[20]

It must be noted that not all the funded libraries participated the full five years. Every year, according to funding available and what colleges were able to meet the financial requirements set forth by the fund, the philanthropic organization made its selections. Those who participated two or three years noted so on their report but still managed to make major progress. It also should be mentioned that a few of the HBCUs were chosen more than once for funding, including A&I State College, CA&N University, West Virginia State College, Virginia Normal & Industrial Institute, Tougaloo College, and Winston-Salem Teachers College.

Black librarianship continued to flourish, and the library and information science (LIS) field began to witness African Americans earning terminal degrees (PhD) in library science. Pioneer Eliza Atkins Gleason (1909–2009) was the first African American to be awarded a PhD in library science from the University of Chicago (1940) where she produced the first comprehensive study of access in Southern libraries.[21] Virginia Lacy Jones (1912–1984)

Year	Number Selected for Funding
1927-1928	5
1928-1929	17
1929-1930	25
Total Grants	47

Number of HBCU libraries funded by the Julius Rosenwald fund, by year.

became the second to receive the doctorate from Chicago in 1945 and later served as the first dean of the Atlanta University School of Library Service (1941–1981).[22] Annette Hoage Phinazee (1920–1983) was the first woman, and first African American, to earn a PhD in information science from Columbia University in 1961 and later served as the first African American president of the North Carolina Library Association.[23] Soon after, Jessie Carney Smith became the first African American to earn a PhD from the University of Illinois at Urbana–Champaign, in 1964, and succeeded Arna Bontemps at Fisk University until her retirement in 2017.[24]

ROSENWALD: INFLUENCER OF LIBRARY PHILANTHROPY

The fund recognized that the Southern region was far too large to approach library development with a blanket solution such as general book service. The organization sought to aid in the overall development of Southern libraries through a combination of approaches. These approaches included: (1) cooperative efforts in increasing the amount of material available and accessible; (2) cooperation in professional training of teachers and librarians; and (3) a cooperative study of regional problems.[25] Though progress was made on monumental levels in the South, the organization understood there would be a limit to what could be done financially and on the service level. A key factor in the philanthropic agency's decision to aid in library development with the tiered approach was to stimulate other libraries, organizations, and philanthropists to contribute to developing Southern libraries for the underserved.

The Rosenwald library sets became increasingly popular, causing high demand from school and county libraries previously unable to afford to build their book collections beyond worn literature. A multitude of schools on various levels were able to obtain funding from external sources, including the state department of education and the local community, to purchase one or more of the fund's library sets. This demand was not limited to the rural schools across the South. Teacher training colleges also requested the library sets to assist in proper training. In 1948, Virginia Lacy Jones requested a large number of children's literature for training teachers and librarians. [26]

The stimulation of book service encouraged other philanthropists to contribute to developing libraries. In 1939, an anonymous black-owned business organization in Washington, D.C., read about the generosity of the fund in the *Wilson Bulletin* and became inspired to gift books about African American life to three poorly equipped black high schools. [27] The operation also encouraged other organizations not previously invested in developing the South to provide reading materials. In 1940, the Los Angeles Schools' Library Textbooks Division gifted more than 3,000 pounds of discarded books in fair condition to 13 Southern states with the fund paying for the cost of freight to each department of education. The division also agreed to continue this service as the books mounted in the storage warehouse. [28] This was an important development for the region as it enabled Georgia, Florida, Virginia, Kentucky, and Arkansas, which were previously ineligible to participate in the library program's experiments and demonstrations, the ability to finally increase their book collections.

The stimulation of book service also motivated other philanthropists and philanthropic organizations to contribute to developing black librarianship. Prior to the closing of Hampton's library school (1939), the Rosenwald Fund, the General Education Board, and the Carnegie Corporation sought a permanent home for the program. Atlanta University and Fisk University were perspective sites, while Hampton was still active. Upon the closing of Hampton's library school and the Rosenwald Fund, a survey was conducted by the dean at Emory University's library school, Tommie Dora Barker, inquiring about the demand for black librarians. Barker concluded two programs were needed: one for paraprofessionals for teacher librarians of secondary schools (known today as library media specialists) and a professional degree-granting program for those aspiring to work in public and academic libraries. Keeping with Rosenwald's example, funding was provided by the General Education Board and the Carnegie Corporation. [29] Additionally, the General Education Board funded the Negro Teacher-Librarian Training program (1936–1939) coordinated by Florence Rising Curtis. The program, credited for training 279 African American teacher-librarians at HBCUs in the South, operated from centers at Atlanta University, Fisk University, Hampton Institute, and Prairie View A&M University. [30]

The library practices at Rosenwald-funded libraries and "non-Rosenwald" libraries dwelled on the same principles and goals focused on literacy and access. The historical materials highlight the importance of the archival analysis. The archival documents revealed an agency created by a man that was determined to assist in diminishing the plight of African Americans through efforts that would increase literacy levels and educational opportunities. Library practices began with small library sets and soon increased to large library sets holding thousands of titles and periodicals to major consideration of library facilitaties. With this grand level of dedication and financial assistance, the library became the heart of the HBCU, freely circulating materials that became the veins of the curriculum for various subjects. In addition, the libraries were established to educate nearby rural counties and states about the benefits of library service. Subsequently, the influence spread throughout the South. Desire for an increase in literature and services occurred in neighboring libraries of schools and universities. Growth in the available books, services, and trained librarians was Rosenwald's goal, and it was well achieved, providing a forever impact on the lives of African American users and the Southern region.

Julius Rosenwald, a critical thinker and known experimental philanthropies, wanted to inspire others to give to the cause of increasing educational opportunities for African Americans and become engulfed in efforts to uplift the culture through literacy. Financial philanthropy was a catalyst to change the library practices at Rosenwald-funded libraries in efforts to influence practices at libraries not provided financial support. This was made apparent with the college division of the library program, which was recorded in the fund's archives as one of the most encouraging projects undertaken for black colleges to date and credited Rosenwald as the man that made it happen. The college division of the Julius Rosenwald Fund Library Program was internally deemed to be the most successful of the experiments and funding given toward libraries. With this radical change, teacher training colleges were able to sufficiently train the next generation of teachers, build book collections that increased by the thousands and covered a variety of topics, build modern libraries and reading rooms, increase the number of trained librarians and library workers, and become pillars of literacy, growth, and development in the black community, contributing to many generations of lifelong learners.

JULIUS ROSENWALD FUND, COLLEGE LIBRARY AID, 1927–1930

The following two pages of information provide details of the Julius Rosenwald Fund, College Library Aid, from 1927 through 1930.

Chapter 4

1927–28

Institution	Rosenwald Aid	Total for Book Purchase
Tuskegee Institute (Alabama)	$500	$1,500
Southern University (Louisiana)	1,000	3,000
Virginia Normal & Industrial Institute (Virginia)	1,000	3,000
A. & I. State College (Tennessee)	2,000	6,000
Winston-Salem Teachers' College (North Carolina)	2,000	6,000
Total	**$6,500**	**$19,500**

1928–29

Institution	Rosenwald Aid	Total for Book Purchase
A. & M. College (South Carolina)	$1,000	$3,000
C. A. & N. University (Oklahoma)	1,000	3,000
Elizabeth City State Normal (North Carolina)	1,000	3,000
Miles Memorial College (Alabama)	1,250	3,750
State Normal (Alabama)	2,500	7,500
State N. & I. Institute (Texas)	1,500	4,500
Kentucky State Industrial College (Kentucky)	1,000	3,000
N. C. College for Negroes (North Carolina)	750	2,250
West Virginia State College (West Virginia)	1,000	3,000
Tougaloo College (Mississippi)	250	750
Bennett College for Women (North Carolina)	1,500	4,500
Virginia Normal and Industrial Institute (Virginia)	1,000 (2nd)	3,000
Mississippi A. & M. College (Mississippi)	2,000	6,000
State College for Colored Students (Delaware)	1,000	3,000
A. & I. State College (Tennessee)	500 (2nd)	1,500
Bluefield Institute (West Virginia)	1,000	3,000
West Virginia State College (West Virginia)	1,500 (2nd)	4,500
Total	**$19,750**	**$59,250**

1929–30

Institution	Rosenwald Aid	Total for Book Purchase
Lane College (Tennessee)	$1,600	$4,800
Selma University (Alabama)	1,000	3,000
Arkansas A. & M. College (Arkansas)	2,500	7,500
Florida A. & M. College (Tallahassee)	2,000	6,000
Ft. Valley High & Industrial (Georgia)	1,000	3,000
Lincoln University (Missouri)	2,500	7,500
N. C. College for Negroes (North Carolina)	1,750 (2nd)	5,250
C. A. & N. University (Oklahoma)	1,000 (2nd)	3,000
Guadalupe College (Texas)	2,500	7,500
Kittrell College (North Carolina)	500	1,500
Morris Brown University (Georgia)	2,500	7,500
Philander Smith College (Arkansas)	2,250	6,750
Rust College (Mississippi)	2,500	7,500
Agricultural & Technical College (North Carolina)	1,250	3,750
Virginia Normal and Industrial Institute (Virginia)	500 (3rd)	1,500
Bethune-Cookman College (Florida)	500	1,500
High School and Junior College (Arkansas)	1,250	3,750
Tougaloo College (Mississippi)	250 (2nd)	750
Livingstone College (North Carolina)	500	1,500
Winston-Salem Teachers' College (North Carolina)	500 (2nd)	1,500
Jackson College (Mississippi)	1,000	3,000
C. A. & N. University (Oklahoma)	500 (3rd)	1,500
Virginia Union University (Virginia)	1,000	3,000
Spelman College (Georgia)	2,500	7,500
Stowe College (Missouri)	1,000	4,000
Total	**$34,350**	**$104,050**
Grand Total	$60,600	$182,800

NOTES

1. S. L. Smith, "The Julius Rosenwald Library Program," *American School Board Journal* (November 1948).
2. Online Computer Library Center (OCLC), "Melville Dewey Biography," https:// www.oclc.org/en/dewey/resources/biography.html/
3. "Edward Christopher Williams," in *Notable Black American Men*, book II, ed. Jessie Carney Smith (Detroit: Gale, 1998).
4. Darlene Clark Hine, ed.,*Black Women in America: An Historical Encyclopedia*, vols. 1 and 2 (Brooklyn: Carlson, 1993).
5. E. Figa and J. Macpherson, *"Brown v. Board of Education* and Its Effect on Libraries and Library and Information Science Education," in *Unfinished Business: Race, Equity and Diversity in Library and Information Science Education* ed. Maurice Wheeler, 3–41 (Lanham, MD: Scarecrow, 2005).
6. Ibid. See also R. DuMont, "The Educating of Black Librarians: An Historical Perspective," *Journal of Education for Library and Information Science* 26, no. 4 (1986): 344–48.
7. See Figa, *"Brown v. Board of Education,"* 11.
8. Emory University desegregation collection, 1960–1994.
9. See DuMont, "Educating of Black Librarians."
10. New York State Library, 94th Annual Report (1911). See also the reports from the archival collections used in the original study. The collections document the activities and in-depth commitment of Curtis.
11. See DuMont, "Educating of Black Librarians."
12. See Southern Association of Colleges and Schools Commission on Colleges, July 2017 list of members and candidates for accreditation, which also notes the initial accreditation date.
13. The U.S. Constitution states, "Congress shall make no law respecting an establishment of religion, or prohibiting the free exercise thereof."
14. Fisk University, John and Aurelia E. Franklin Library, Special Collections, S. L. Smith Collection, box 42, folder 5.
15. Ibid.
16. Ibid.
17. Fisk University, John and Aurelia E. Franklin Library, Special Collections, Julius Rosenwald Fund Archives, box 261, folder 5.
18. Ibid.
19. Ibid.
20. Fisk University, John and Aurelia E. Franklin Library, Special Collections, S. L. Smith Collection, box 8, folder 8.
21. University of Illinois, College of Arts and Sciences Hall of Honor, accessed June 3, 2019, https://las.illinois.edu.
22. Virginia Lacy Jones papers, 1912–1985, Atlanta University Center.
23. B. F. Speller, "Alethia Annette Lewis Hoage Phinazee (1920–1983)," in *Dictionary of American Library Biography*, vol. 3, ed. D. G. Dai, 173–74 (Westport, CT: Libraries Unlimited, 2003).
24. "Jessie Carney Smith: Biography," *The HistoryMakers*, April 22, 2014, https:// www.thehistorymakers.org/biography/jessie=carney=smith. I worked at Fisk University during an IMLS fellowship as archivist (2011–2012) and later as head of Special Collections and Archives (2013–2015).
25. See Louis Wilson and Edward Wight's report *County Library Service in the South: A Study of the Rosenwald County Library Demonstration* (Chicago: University of Chicago Press, 1935).
26. Fisk University, John and Aurelia E. Franklin Library, Special Collections, Julius Rosenwald Fund Archives, box 88, folder 1.
27. Fisk University, John and Aurelia E. Franklin Library, Special Collections, Julius Rosenwald Fund Archives, box 129, folder 3.
28. Fisk University, John and Aurelia E. Franklin Library, Special Collections, Julius Rosenwald Fund Archives, box 259, folder 10.

29. Eliza Atkins Gleason, "The Atlanta University School of Library Service: Its Aims and Objectives," *Library Quarterly* 12, no. 3 (July 1942): 504–10. See also Risa L. Mulligan, "The Closing of the Clark Atlanta University School of Library and Information Studies" (master's thesis, University of North Carolina at Chapel Hill, 2006).

30. "Negro Teacher-Librarian Training Program (1936–1939): A Brief Historical Overview," Prairie View A&M University, accessed June 3, 2019, http://www.pvamu.edu/library/about-the-library/history-of-the-library-at-prarie-view/negro-tacher-librarian-training-program-1936-1939.

Chapter Five

Community Outreach in Motion

The concept of community outreach is based on an organization's goal to provide a service to a population that otherwise would not have access. The Rosenwald Fund conducted community outreach for African Americans in the American South during a time when development was emotionally and financially stalled for the entire rural area. The initial decade was devoted to building schoolhouses for African Americans in 15 Southern states. While subsequent years focused on areas that promoted literacy for increased educational opportunities with the abilities to span across generations, under the authority of Edwin R. Embree and the board of trustees, operations now encompassed fellowships and scholarships, healthcare and medical service, library service, education, social studies, race relations, and rural education. [1]

FELLOWSHIPS AND SCHOLARSHIPS

One of the lesser-known activities of the fund is the financial support for promising individuals through fellowships and scholarships. With thousands of rural schools established for African Americans, officers of the fund aimed to honor Julius Rosenwald's instructions to spend down all available funds within 25 years of his death. The administrators concentrated on causes that would uphold the Rosenwald legacy and provide a greater impact. Though the philanthropist had not made formal plans to provide financial assistance to individuals as he had focused on the improvement of entire communities, no one could deny that the school-building program and libraries changed countless lives and the entire Southern region. Despite the growth in educational opportunities for blacks, minority scholars met a number of financial hindrances to adequately compete against white counterparts who were given greater resources. The vaster resources came with institutional and/or organizational affiliation deemed more prestigious compared to that of the early 20th-century black college.[2]

The foundation of fellowships, though unofficial, began with Rosenwald and African American biologist Ernest E. Just. The Howard University professor was highly regarded in national and international arenas for his work. Still, he lacked the financial resources necessary for research and travel. There are conflicting accounts of how the biologist came to know Rosenwald. On one account, Just was referred by Abraham Flexner, then associated with the Rockefeller Foundation. For reasons unknown, Flexner was not able to provide support through the Rockefeller Foundation and referred him to Rosenwald.[3] Another narrative credits Just for contacting the United States' National Research Council, which then referred him to Rosenwald. Prior to this contact, the philanthropist had not provided financial support to an individual not based on organizational affiliation.[4] The scholar shared his life with Rosenwald and the struggles of being an African American academician. This was a problem not restricted to the sciences but an attribute of living in the Jim Crow era where race was a place card for assigned seats. His authentic appeal to the philanthropist resulted in funded research. Though the university administration did not label Just's work as an asset, they also did not want the professor to resign from his teaching duties. In exchange for Flexner securing a large donation for the university from the Rockefeller Foundation, the school officials agreed to reduce Just's workload.[5] The year was 1920 when Rosenwald started the inaugural fellowship, awarding the biologist $2,000 per year for three years, though the financial support would cover a total of seven years.[6]

Proposed by President Embree to the board of trustees, the fellowship program was governed by a committee consisting of Embree, Will Winston Alexander, Charles Spurgeon Johnson, and Henry Allen Moe. The notable group of gentlemen initially focused on the short-term training that would advance the studies of black students using the instrumentalist approach that Rosenwald followed closely and that was presented by his dear friend Booker T. Washington. The program would honor the intentions of increasing the number of black African American staff members and participants in areas and agencies, which the fund had vested interest in assisting the community in uplift.

Between 1928 and 1936, the Julius Rosenwald Fund granted nearly 400 fellowships of almost half a million dollars to librarians and library administrators, physicians and nurses, and Urban League administrators. In addition, 18 scholarships for completion of scholarly works were granted within this time frame.[7] The strides the students were making were remarkable. Regarding a 1931 letter from Mary E. Hunter, who excitedly wrote to Embree to inform him that she had received her master of science in home economics (the first black woman to accomplish such a feat at Iowa State College), he noted, "When Negroes have the ability (beyond question) they sweep aside all barriers. It may be as well that Negro students have to be extra good. That forces a selection process."[8]

Following the doctrine of W. E. B. DuBois, perhaps unknowingly, members of the fellowship committee were gradualists who desired to emphasize the division. They sought evolutionary change in race relations—ultimately integration. The formalized program began to see a shift away from Rosenwald's approach with the addition of a fourth category for the fellowships and grants-in-aid that focused on creative and fine arts.[9] Though Embree may not have intended to completely abandon the instrumentalist method, he did aim to contribute to the production of African American educational leadership, effectively establishing a black social and cultural elite, which DuBois details the necessity for in his 1903 article "The Negro Problem." In the article, solidifying the concept of the talented tenth, the renowned scholar contended that the Negro race would be saved by African Americans with standards of excellence, leadership, and superior performance. He noted the necessity for blacks to have equal opportunity for classic, formal education that went beyond industrial training. This doctrine celebrated the exceptional minds of the black community that would be the light that uplifts the entire culture. The fellowship committee members strongly believed this uplift would also reduce racial attitudes with aspirations to diminish the threat of blacks felt by whites. With the support of black elites, including Charles Spurgeon Johnson and James Weldon Johnson, advocating for black artists pre- and post Harlem Renaissance, Embree's proposal was influential.[10] The Harlem Renaissance and the artists who built the cultural movement set the stage for creative African Americans who used visual and audible ways of expression to present authentic messages of racial struggle and hope for triumph. The white community demonstrated empathy and became a key actor in a midcentury social movement for equality.[11]

Between 1936 and 1942, the fund provided 234 fellowships that went to 131 African Americans, while 101 went to whites.[12] African Americans focused on areas of sociology, language and literature, fine arts, economics, and history. The fund and the committee demonstrated its commitment to the noninstrumentalist approach, whether highlighting elite scholars with a "honor roll of great distinction" for exceptional candidates or revealing their preference for the liberal curriculum through the selection process. The board of trustees began to shift to become more inclusive in the distribution of fellowships. With the start of World War II, the number of fellowships declined; however, the number of women applicants increased significantly. During wartime, democratic values questioned the concept of segregation as well as gender traditions. The war became a gateway for social change where the job shortage caused blacks and whites to physically work together, and women to step into the role of providers and seek opportunities outside of the home as husband and fathers were away at war. There was no turning back, no need to return to a time that held the region from steadily progressing as the North had decades prior.

The fellowship's program was beyond supporting advance training to increase educational opportunities. Yes, there was an increase in classical education for hundreds who needed the financial assistance to simply compete with white counterparts. However, arguably the greatest impact that the program contributed was the transition of ideology from Washington's doctrine that focused on industrial education, emphasizing the way for the black community to develop themselves, to DuBois's talented tenth that acknowledged the need for a class of black social and cultural elite and developing a cohort for black educational leadership. No argument will be made here concerning the superiority of the Washington and DuBois doctrines and the level of benefits to the fellowship program and the black community. Instead, the stance will be taken that both doctrines were necessary to develop education for the black community and social change in America.

HEALTHCARE AND MEDICAL SERVICES

The healthcare needs of blacks were often aligned with the educational void. The mortality rate among blacks was reported at 17.6 percent in 1924, which was higher than the rest of the population at 11.8 percent. Various contributing factors, including lack of access to hospitals, trained professionals, and disease prevention services, fueled the community's economic disadvantage and increased exposure to industrial risks. During 1927, the Rosenwald Fund launched its health program to assist in closing the gap in healthcare disparities within the black community with acknowledgment that it would take far more than one organization could reasonably hope to assume full responsibility of the immense health needs for a tenth of the American people.

When the healthcare program began, there was limited or no access to hospital facilities that serviced blacks, due to not only the Jim Crow era but also the restricted number of black healthcare professionals who were properly trained. To stimulate the employment of public health nurses by state and county health departments, the fund paid a part of their salaries over a five-year period with the understanding that the local health departments would assume full financial responsibility at the close of the funding period. Upon the start of the healthcare program, fund officials noted that to their knowledge there was not a single black nurse employed by public authorities in the entire South. With this initiative, more than 300 black nurses were appointed and publicly supported.[13] In addition, the fund addressed the needed reduction in maternal and infant mortality by training black nurses at Tuskegee in proper birthing techniques. Established in 1941 with the cooperation of the Federal Children's Bureau as well as state and county authorities, this was the first school designed to educate African American nurses in maternal and infant welfare.

The organization had a special interest in developing black hospitals, providing demonstrations in excellent medical care and establishing centers that granted advanced education to minority physicians and nurses. By 1940, there were 110 "Negro" hospitals in the United States, of which 25 had been granted the proper accreditation and were 13 approved to train interns by the Council on Medical Education and Hospitals of the American Hospital Association. During the evaluation year, 10,000 hospital beds were available to blacks in the United States. However, some areas with a heavier black population hosted as few as 75 beds, allowing for health facilities and services to be at an overall disadvantage. [14] A main source of this matter was the lack of black professionals employed at the local or state levels based on the as-

Group of African American midwives during a maternal and infant welfare program in Virginia, April 22, 1930. *Fisk University, John Hope and Aurelia E. Franklin Library, Special Collections, Julius Rosenwald Fund Collection, supplement 2, series 7, photographs, box 24F.*

sumption that the African American community was not interested in wellness as a career. Thus, the fund sought to establish black physicians as qualified for employment and service in the high-level capacity for public agencies. Without reluctance, the organization temporarily covered the cost of advanced education for physicians and health officers in an effort to involve black males in health-based government projects.

The fund made special efforts to demonstrate the feasibility of controlling chief causes of sickness and death among blacks. Funding prioritized research in the treatment of tuberculosis and syphilis. One of the greatest handicaps to detecting disease at an early stage was the inflated cost for exams, including skin testing, X-rays, and properly trained professionals to analyze any findings. The fund cooperated with the University of Chicago's Provident Hospital to experiment with effective methods of identifying tuberculosis in its early stages. In addition, in collaboration with the National Tuberculosis Association, the fund established a committee focused on disease control in the African American community with $63,000 to work with local public and private organizations. The fund's commitment to health improvements for the black community and tax-supported medical and health services allowed for noticeable changes that began to take place. With diligence, the tuberculosis mortality rate dropped from 235 per 100,000 in 1920 to an estimated 129 per 100,000 by 1928.[15]

The Julius Rosenwald Fund was one of many organizations that became intimately involved in the uplift of the African American culture, and for Embree that was not limited to schoolhouses. He bravely attacked various matters affecting this community, understanding the overall benefits that would reach across cultures. This foundation was one of the most involved and influential private organizations that collaborated with others to produce effective success for the large region.[16] The Julius Rosenwald Fund allocated more than $1.4 million to health and medical services for African Americans.[17] Embree provided the general strategy for the healthcare program initiative designed for the black community. He sought to (1) enlist the assistance and prestige of the U.S. Public Health Service to stimulate and extend the interest of health departments and other agencies concerning the needs of blacks and make practical steps toward accommodating them, in addition to seeking out the National Tuberculosis Association and the National Organization for Public Health Nursing to supplement the services; (2) aid in increasing the number of hospitals that offered healthcare services to African Americans as well as the ability to demonstrate high standards for operations and training for black physicians, nurses, and administrators; (3) encourage the use of health departments and voluntary agencies of black physicians and nurses, particularly those who specialize in public health and assist in establishing adequate training; and (4) develop practical methods of

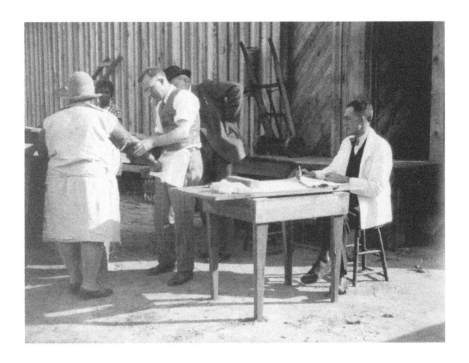

1932 syphilis campaign. A medical expert provides the Wassermann test while the efficiency expert takes notes. *Fisk University, John Hope and Aurelia E. Franklin Library, Special Collections, Julius Rosenwald Fund Archives, 1917–1948, box 558, folder 7.*

health education for school teachers, schoolchildren, and communities according to policies and levels of expense suited to Southern conditions.

The development of 16 hospitals and clinics widely distributed throughout the country is a notable accomplishment. These hospitals successfully positioned themselves to offer postgraduate instruction and experience to physicians and other healthcare workers. The employment of black nurses who specialized in public health exceeded expectations and established a considerable amount of healthcare practices in Northern and Southern cities. Reluctant campaigns against tuberculosis and syphilis proved financially feasibile to control and aimed to prevent such plagues. Furthermore, officials were committed to increasing appropriation for public health specifically against these diseases. In the control of contagious diseases, it became especially clear that the well-being of the whole population is dependent on the health of each group, not just African Americans.[18]

Throughout the eight years of work in healthcare and medical services, the primary goal was to make good medical care more widely available to

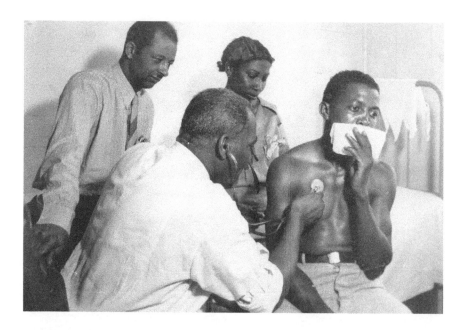

At the Tuberculosis Institute for Negro Physicians in Miami, Florida, July 6–31, 1936, Dr. A. J. Kershaw examines a patient while Dr. L. H. B. Foote, medical director at Florida A&M University, and medical nurse Willie Mae Bailey observe. *Fisk University, John Hope and Aurelia E. Franklin Library, Special Collections, Julius Rosenwald Fund Archives, 1917–1948, box 558, folder 7.*

persons of moderate and low incomes. Fund officials studied and encouraged the creation of health plans that would make it possible for people to budget the unpredictable cost of illness through insurance or taxation and plans that reduced the cost of medical care and improved its quality by better organizing professional services. The methods to improve healthcare included the following:

- Studies of economic, administrative, and social aspects of medical services
- Studies and appraisals of new plans and experiments in group payment and in organized medical services
- Advisory and consultant services to professional groups, community agencies, and medical institutions with respect to existing or proposed plans
- Financial aid for a few select plans and experiments
- Dissemination of the fund's studies and reports and additional information to physicians, professional groups, and the public concerning the social and economic aspects of medical service

- Consultation and conference with other agencies active in the coordination of work and an effective division of labor

The fund's officers took on substantial tasks to ensure success; they (a) assumed a substantial part in the initiation, organization, and research of the committee on the cost of medical care; (b) collaborated and cooperated with other foundations and agencies in the distribution of the committee's studies and reports; (c) participated with the American Hospital Association in developing voluntary insurance for hospital care, which was established in more than 60 cities; (d) performed studies concerning financial and community uncertainties about hospitals through the American Hospital Association and education in hospitals for administration through the University of Chicago; (e) conducted studies and executed practical public health programs, rural hospitals, and public medical care through participation in the work of the president's committee on economic security, United States Public Health Service, and voluntary agencies; and (f) were influential in the work of foundations and other organizations interested in medical economics.[19] A study of trends (1930–1939) in public health activities related to the African American community was created under the auspices of the Julius Rosenwald Fund in 1940 through a grant to Howard University College of Medicine.

RACE RELATIONS INSTITUTE

The racially driven, yet progressive decade of the 1940s presented a plethora of opportunities ignited by the Harlem Renaissance. Among those catalysts were the Fair Employment Practices Committee, the Tuskegee Air Squadron, the Congress of Racial Equality (CORE), and 1948's Executive Order 9981, signed by President Truman.[20] The South required continuous and consistent progress toward racial equality on the grassroots level. Fisk University took on this task with a scholarly approach when it established the Race Relations Department, a collaborative effort among the Julius Rosenwald Fund, the American Missionary Association, and the social science department at Fisk University in 1942.

Charles Spurgeon Johnson (1893–1956), a respected sociologist and authority on race relations studies, played a vital role in securing the department for the university. Prior to venturing to Nashville, Johnson was a recognized force with research planted in rectifying race relations in America. A graduate of Virginia Union University, he was the understudy of profound scholar Robert Ezra Park at the University of Chicago. After completing the apprentice-like experience, he worked for the Chicago Commission on Race Relations (1919–1921).[21] Subsequently, Johnson accepted the task of directing research for the National Urban League, where he established the notable periodical *Opportunity: Journal of Negro Life*, which provided a voice for participants and supporters of the Harlem Renaissance. Along with other featured scholars, Johnson was a leader in literary arts and focused his sociological studies on race relations. The educator joined the Fisk faculty in 1928 as the chair of the social science department. Johnson wasted no time in his lifelong commitment to improve race relations with the creation of prominent studies that investigated cities where racial tensions took permanent residence, and he published books on race relations for laymen and conducted a number of sponsored surveys on race.[22]

The importance of the work performed within Fisk's social science department became more crucial with the onset of war, where men had to rely on each other to survive but faced issues of stereotypes and trust. With uncertainty concerning the war's aftermath, a number of organizations sought to assist veterans returning home. The Rosenwald Fund took notice of this need for information and provided military bases and hospitals with literature covering the contributions of blacks to American society as well as the works of notable literary figures. As servicemen and women ventured home, the demand for manpower propelled millions of people to migrate into the industrial workforce with existing racial tensions and attitudes toward blacks due to lack of exposure and years of segregation, allowing for preconceived notions to heightened. We should not forget the discriminatory conditions and practices during war that contributed toward the nation's racial divide. Developmental and philanthropic organizations desired to avoid a racially fueled aftermath such as that of post–World War I, which led the American Missionary Association to establish a Race Relations Department at Fisk University.

During late spring 1942, leadership of the American Missionary Association (AMA) decided it was necessary for the association to focus on the issue of race relations, particularly focusing on relationships between blacks and whites.[23] In a cooperative effort, Fred L. Brownlee of the American Missionary Association, President Thomas Elsa Jones of Fisk University, and Edwin R. Embree of the Julius Rosenwald Fund agreed to jointly use Charles S. Johnson's services in the field of race relations. The leaders appointed Johnson as the director of the race relations division of the American Missionary Association, effective January 1, 1943, with an annual salary of $2,500. Though his core salary was covered by the AMA, he was also compensated by the Rosenwald Fund and Fisk University. The AMA also funded all of Johnson's housing costs in New York and Chicago.[24] The fund sponsored a number of the studies and compensated Johnson for his work. The newly appointed director agreed to provide access to all reports to the AMA and the fund as a measure of extending influence into local communities to reduce racial tensions. Johnson experienced high demand due to his experience, knowledge, and openness to directly address all matters of race. He rendered services to other organizations with similar goals, such as the Tennessee Valley Authority, the United States Department of Labor, and the State of Louisiana Department of Education, among other state and federal departments. Unfortunately, the university could not solely maintain the cost of the department. The fund and AMA stepped in to provide financial support in order to continue the important work because this was a mutually beneficial relationship among three organizational administrations.

The department was also successful in developing studies for publication for external organizations and communities, including manuals, pamphlets, studies, and monthly reports, as well as free and paid subscriptions aimed to reduce and eliminate matters related to racial aggressions. Publications were a smaller, yet effective method to educate audiences, though it was only a start to the department's efforts toward mass education. Between 1943 and 1948, the fund, race relations division of the AMA, and American Council of Race Relations made monthly contributions toward the cost of publications for ongoing studies on race relations in the United States.

Efforts put forth by Johnson on behalf of Fisk, the AMA, and the fund played a vital role in reducing stereotypes that fueled racial tensions toward African Americans, who as a group were reasonably guarded. However, the intention of the program's design did not aim to eliminate the issue of poor race relations, which reflected American politics, specifically that of the South. Though these politics were slow to change, revolution required facilitation, which was the department's aim. In fall 1943, the director presented the program's nine goals and objectives:

1. To define the problem areas in race relations soundly, and in such a manner as to make programs of action comprehensively possible
2. To develop, from the best-known experiences in the field, courses of constructive action in special areas that can be usefully employed by agencies and persons in other areas
3. To develop soundly resourceful persons capable of meeting and dealing with new situations in an acceptable manner
4. To develop materials for public education in race relations, using the most effective channels of communications: press, radio, visual devices, and school curriculum
5. To work in geographic areas of racial tension, with the view to using local resources to prevent overt racial clashes
6. To plan systematically for the community handling of anticipated racial problems resulting from general economic, social, or political emergencies
7. To develop new areas of racial appreciation, understanding, and common responsibility

8. To aid in developing programs of racial democracy within the church, labor organizations, and youth groups
9. To develop with the institutional structure of the school programs of democratic understanding and practice, as one of the essential functions of public education[25]

With the outbreak of ongoing race riots in rural and industrial cities, field-workers were positioned and equipped to established local programs designed to relieve racial tensions and help others acknowledge economic issues affecting the black community. Much like the Rosenwald Fund, Johnson understood that opportunities were the concrete solution for advancement, education, and employment. The staff was expanded to include an expert on industrial workforce and the reduction of segregated plants.

Johnson consistently displayed a prestigious level of leadership, resulting in an offer to be the president of the historic institution. In fall 1946, Johnson became Fisk University's first black president and selected Herman Long as his successor for the Race Relations Department. The department continued to produce effective studies under the leadership of Long, including a "self-study" examining the involvement of local authorities to address and resolve racial issues such as disparities in socioeconomics, education, employment, and housing. Such studies highlighted the importance of community involvement with local politics to effectively address the imbalance in resource distribution. Though the program's stated purpose to address racial tensions focused on discriminatory practices toward African Americans, the department was often criticized for conducting a self-study and not focusing on multiple minority groups. With closer examination, skeptics would find that other cultures were also invested in improving conditions for blacks, including various Jewish organizations. They also saw uplifting this hindered culture, specifically in the South, as a key mechanism for reducing race-based divisions. This could be considered a form of social intervention. The department demonstrated the importance of involving local community members as a way to indicate their desire for restoration and value as they have a vested interest in better integration of African Americans into American society. The department solidified the approach of the self-study, despite minimum staff. The impact, as well as visibility, increased with the creation of annual programs.

Johnson created in 1944 the Race Relations Institute, a small conference held on the Fisk University campus during the summer. He envisioned it as an extended professional meeting with individual papers and discussions. In fact, the three-week symposium would become the primary identity of the department and solidified Fisk University as the center for research in field investigations concerning race relations. The institute concentrated its purpose on providing practical, intensive studies of complications associated with discrimination in labor relations, media, education, and community. The inaugural institute boasted more than 180 attendees consisting of educators, college students, civic leaders, and social workers. Set up in the style of the modern-day professional conference with panels and discussions from leaders in various fields, it was conservative yet calculated. It was because of Johnson and others like him that the institution was successful and resulted in a scholarly tradition. In an effort to support the next conference, the subsequent three-week program attached a $55 fee. The institute covered the matters of race relations on a variety of levels, including those of government. Vibrant discussions often centered on the role of federal agencies to determine race-based policies in labor and employment, local housing, community adjustment of black migrants to urban areas, and the adjustment of returning black veterans. At the conclusion of the conference, leaders would examine the role of the press in education, transportation, and the prospects for the postwar economy. The three-week institute became an academic, scholarly, and economic commitment to all issues related to race in America and worldwide. The conference experience increased attendance and managed to balance the political, economic, and social matters specifically in the South. Despite controversial discussions, Fisk University president Charles Johnson continued to provide an opening address to acknowledge the purpose. The participation of notable historical figures such as Thurgood Marshall and Martin Luther King Jr. provided additional validation to the annual platform that supported civil rights as human rights.

Shortly after the *Brown v. Board* decision of 1954, which found segregation in public schools unconstitutional, the annual program found Johnson excitedly and prematurely announcing that the need for such institutions would cease.[26] Unfortunately, the intellect was no fortune-teller. While the Supreme Court's decision may have influenced the increased attendance of the institute, it also created the desire to move the conversation toward addressing those experiences of other cultures, specifically postwar.[27] This is something Johnson attempted to discuss during various programs and publications. However, the institute was created to focus on the issues of blacks in America, a topic the 1960s would make evident. The Race Relations Institute remained a relevant model for contemporary civil rights in social justice activism until the civil rights movement became an institution of its own, teaching the world the crucial need to fight for equality while using America as a case study. The media attention from Northern involvement not only highlighted the countless injustices toward the black community but also uprooted the end of the three-week conference. America was now more aware of its racial problems than ever before, and it could not be denied because the civil rights movement was an "in your face" fight for human rights, calling for the institute to change its pace or come to a close. As the social movement inspired grassroots activism across the South and discriminatory practices dominated media coverage, many leaders became absent as fieldwork was priority. A year and two months past the tragic assassination of Martin Luther King, Fisk held the final Race Relations Institute (June 1969). Many seats of notable civil rights leaders were vacant; however, Roy Wilkins and Fannie Lou Hamer participated in the final discussions.[28] Though Johnson dies at the age of 63, his legacy was already engraved in history, notably for the Race Relations Institute and his presidency at Fisk University.

Fund officials sought to greatly affect and uplift a culture that was at a disadvantage by design. Financial contributions made in the form of fellowships and scholarships gave nearly 400 promising individuals the opportunity to achieve scholarly successes. An increase in healthcare offerings was implemented to enhance access to medical services, properly trained black medical professionals, and training facilities. The annual programs, publications, and fieldwork activities conducted by the Race Relations Institute established some of the groundwork for the forthcoming civil rights movement. Though overall progress in the Jim Crow South was hindered due to the curse of racism, fund officers diligently worked against the norm of oppressing the African American community by creating countless opportunities for the recipients and generations to follow. The social, political, and economic issues that the Julius Rosenwald Fund identified as crucial disparities in the early 20th century became traditions of a narrative and an entire academic discipline, recognized by today's scholars and politicians as continuous race-based obstacles in the 21st century.

* * *

On the next page is an appendix listing available fellowships.

APPENDIX: FELLOWSHIPS

Subject	Number Granted	Total
Agriculture	43	$48,226
The Arts (Painting, sculpture, dramatics)	6	12,060
Music	28	34,485
Literature	7	24894
Accounting and Business Administration	14	6,384
Education	12	12478
Home Economics	33	27,876
Library Administration	34	32,100
Physical Sciences (Chemistry, Physics, Mathematics, Engineering)	16	12,881
Biology and Medical Sciences	6	6,644
Social Sciences	27	31,360
Medicine and Surgery	45	68,946
Nursing	24	14,397
Hospital Administration and Health Services	13	8,023
Liberal Arts	18	11,069
Law	3	1,800
Social Work	40	29,189
Trades and Vocational Guidance	20	14,310
	389	$397122
Grants-in-aid and special payments	18	$40,493
Total		$437,615

NOTES

1. E. Embree, *Julius Rosenwald Fund, 1917–1936* (Chicago: Chicago University Press, 1936). Embree was president of the Julius Rosenwald Fund, 1927–1948. He previously worked with the Rockefeller Foundation (ca. 1917–1927). This is also the source for the appendix, "Fellowships."

2. This was also a matter of the institution having available funds to support its faculty. Historically, black colleges were underfunded.

3. M. Werner, *Julius Rosenwald: The Life of a Practical Humanitarian* (New York: Harper, 1939).

4. J. R. Nolting, *The Julius Rosenwald Fellowship Program for African American Visual Artists, 1929 to 1948* (Cincinnati, OH: University of Cincinnati Press, 2012), 6.

5. M. Rose, *Rosenwald: The Remarkable Story of a Jewish Partnership with African-American Communities*, dir. Aviva Kempner (Waltham, MA: National Center for Jewish Film, 2013).

6. The research grant of $1,500 was provided, as well as an additional $500 for summer research.

7. Fisk University, John and Aurelia E. Franklin Library, Special Collections, Julius Rosenwald Fund Archives, box 374, folder A. See also the appendix, "Fellowships."

8. Jayne R. Beilke, "The Changing Emphasis of the Rosenwald Fellowship Program, 1928–1948," *Journal of Negro Education* 66, no. 1 (1997): 3–15.

9. Ibid., 9.

10. Scholar and educator Charles S. Johnson was the first African American president of Fisk University and founder of the Race Relations Department at Fisk University. Songwriter and educator James Weldon Johnson penned (alongside his brother, Rosamond) the Negro national anthem, "Lift Ev'ry Voice and Sing."

11. This movement, known as the civil right movement, would present itself on a national scale in 1954.

12. Beilke, "Changing Emphasis of the Rosenwald Fellowship Program," 11.

13. E. Embree, *The Julius Rosenwald Fund: The Review for the Two-Year Period 1938–1940* (Chicago: Rosenwald Fund, 1940), 40.

14. Ibid., 11.

15. Ibid., 11–12.

16. M. L. Banning, *The Contribution of the Julius Rosenwald Fund to Negro Education and Better Race Relations* (PhD diss., University of Arizona, 1945).

17. Embree, *Julius Rosenwald Fund, 1917–1936*, 36, 40.

18. Ibid., 37.

19. Ibid., 41.

20. This executive order desegregated the armed forces.

21. Robert Ezra Park (1864–1944) is regarded as one of the most influential figures in American sociology. His work on human ecology, race relations, migration, assimilation, social movements, and social disorganization connected him to influential figures such as Booker T. Washington. He shared his wealth of knowledge at universities, including Harvard, Tuskegee, and Fisk. While at the University of Chicago, Johnson penned *The Negro in Chicago*, a study on the race riot of 1919. A number of articles credit that study as the literary piece that verified Johnson as an authority in race relations.

22. P. J. Gilpin, "Charles S. Johnson and the Race Relations Institutes at Fisk University," *Phylon (1960–)* 41, no. 3 (1980): 300–311.

23. K. W. Berry, *Charles S. Johnson, Fisk University, and the Struggle for Civil Rights, 1945–1970* (PhD diss., Florida State University, 2005).

24. Ibid., 64–65.

25. Ibid., 69.

26. As we acknowledge, today there remains a need to address race relations in similar aspects with inclusion of discussions on other minority groups, police brutality, mass incarceration, women as leaders of social movements, minorities against each other, and more.

27. Berry, *Charles S. Johnson*, 94–95.

28. Roy Wilkins was then the former director of the NAACP, and Fannie Lou Hamer was then the vice chair of the Mississippi Freedom Democratic Party.

Chapter Six

Philanthropy as Purpose

Philanthropy in the 1920s varied from large monetary donations of philanthropic organizations to small charitable gifts from individuals. No matter the amount, the consideration applied in monetary form was impactful. The nature in which anything is given weighs equally, if not more, but to expect some sort of good karma from the universe defeats the purpose of charity. American Jewish philanthropy is a fusion of Jewish religious traditions and the democratic pluralistic traditions of the United States. Biblical injunctions task those able to protect the poor, orphans, widows, and strangers. The Jewish cultural tradition of "taking care of one's own" shaped philanthropic mechanisms created to address immigrant needs at the turn of the century. Maimonides defines eight levels in giving *tzedakah* (charity), each one higher than the preceding one. On an ascending level, they are as follows:

8. When donations are given grudgingly.

7. When one gives less than he should, but does so cheerfully.

6. When one gives directly to the poor upon being asked.

5. When one gives directly to the poor without being asked.

4. Donations when the recipient is aware of the donor's identity, but the donor still does not know the specific identity of the recipient.

3. Donations when the donor is aware to whom the charity is being given, but the recipient is unaware of the source.

2. Giving assistance in such a way that the giver and recipient are unknown to each other. Communal funds, administered by responsible people, are also in this category.

1. The highest form of Jewish charity is to help sustain people *before* they become impoverished by offering a substantial gift in a dignified manner, extending a suitable loan, or helping them find employment or establishing

themselves in business so as to make it unnecessary for them to become dependent on others. [1]

The two highest levels of giving are often also anonymous and explain why Rosenwald avoided fanfare for his work, especially for the black colleges and libraries. He supplemented the traditional Jewish approach to charity with modern business practices and progressive ideals. Beyond the school-building program, he looked for organizations and persons that would fill the needs in ways that empowered recipients.

ROSENWALD'S PRINCIPLES OF PUBLIC GIVING

Examining Julius Rosenwald's journey of philanthropy and the detailed considerations he took concerning each endeavor, one could define a few key principles of public giving he personally followed. One of the first noted principles would be his experimentation with giving, never committing a large amount until he was convinced his contribution would be of public benefit. This often happened in the form of one-year trials beginning with the rural school project, then libraries, historically black colleges and universities, and so on. In each of these cases, Rosenwald sought to empower the community as it was not his intention to give indefinitely or create an endowment for sustainability. These were social problems that the local community had to be invested in as it was their burden that garnered his initial attention. This highlighted another principle that giving money in general was void whereas effective giving had to be directed toward a positive result, a particular cause. The saying goes, you can give a man a fish, or you can teach him how to fish. A financial handout is temporary, but training or even guidance will stretch much further and empower those in need.

Rosenwald aimed to entice other individuals and organizations with his own financial investment toward a worthy cause (principle 3) that would call for the masses to resolve or affect greatly to a point of stability. This was demonstrated by the stipulations placed in rural schools, libraries, colleges, and financial contributions to organizations, as well as when he worked with the General Education Board, the American Library Association, countless national organizations, and local communities. He knew that the emotional investment had to cross boundaries as he could not financially bear the social justice of mankind. He could not bear this burden due to his most important principle that no charitable organization should exist as a perpetual endowment. He found this vain of men and furthermore misguided when they have a specific purpose as it was more important to give toward present needs.

ORGANIZED PHILANTHROPY:
EXIST IN PERPETUITY OR SUNSET

The second half of the 1920s found the fund flourishing. In April 1928 through September 1929, the trustees appropriated more than $5 million, and the market value of securities soared from $20 million to $35 million.[2] This was a major increase on paper of three times as much as the trustees had appropriated. However, October 1929 would place America in the midst of an unwanted revolution compared to that of the roaring, prosperous 1920s. The economic plague that was the Great Depression, caused by the crash of the stock market, affected countless households and businesses worldwide. More precisely, from 1929 to 1933, the unemployment rate in the United States soared from 3.2 percent to 24.9 percent. More unfortunate, a number of industrial cities more than doubled this number with unemployment as high as 80 percent. During the economic depression, consumer spending declined 18 percent, manufacturing productivity dropped 54 percent, and construction spending plummeted 78 percent. In addition, 80 percent of production capacity in the automobile industry came to a halt.[3] Philanthropy was slowed and in most cases halted due to restricted or a complete lack of funds. In 1932, while serving as the chairman of Sears, Julius Rosenwald passed away, leaving behind his wife and five children: Lessing, Adele, Edith, Marion, and William. His loss of life was significant in many ways, as he had devoted his time, effort, and financial support toward building opportunities that would revolutionize public schools, colleges and universities, museums, Jewish charities, and black institutions.[4]

The Great Depression became an unexpected opportunity/requirement for the fund, and other philanthropic organizations, to reformulate in the wake of financial crisis. With the reality of the market collapse, the fund experienced its own financial crisis. The fund's stock reserve plummeted, leaving the agency facing the harsh possibility of bankruptcy. Edwin R. Embree secured a loan of $1.2 million from the First National Bank of Chicago along with a $200,000 gift from the Carnegie Corporation to cosponsor the fund's library program, a bit more than $69,000 from the Rosenwald Family Association (operated by the founder's children) to resolve the commitments to the Museum of Science and Industry and the American Society for Jewish Farm Settlements, and contributions from individuals such as Theodore Max Troy of Jacksonville, Florida, who gifted $20,195.[5] The Rockefeller Foundation denied Embree's appeal for aid once it concluded the fund's debt was due to fiscal irresponsibility.[6]

One could argue that this rejection was to spite the founder's outspoken stance against foundations existing in perpetuity. The debate of perpetuity versus sunset (also known as spending down) is based on the survival of the donor/founder's initial intent in establishing the organization. Foundations that live in perpetuity can be easily driven by self-interest and/or job security of its trustees, employees, and advisors. Though most private foundations of the early 20th century were organized as perpetual endowments, the concept has not been spared from criticism. Embree speaks of Rosenwald's concern over a bureaucratic and reactionary attitude that may develop by trustees of large endowments held in perpetuity. He opposed the influence of the "dead hand in philanthropy or human affairs." Rosenwald felt by not existing in perpetuity, the current and future generations should provide for their needs that may arise.[7]

Rosenwald was concerned for multiple reasons; the greatest worry was that donors conceived that money given for philanthropic purposes had to be given for a specific objective or in perpetuity, placing a limit on the possibilities prior to the donation. This means the principal donation was to remain untouched, while only the profit or additional income that was gained was to be spent on charitable causes. This is a fast-track method for organizations and institutions to become "endowment poor," where millions of dollars are held in treasuries but only 4 or 5 percent per year is allocated. This actually leaves the institution limited or unable to meet its philanthropic goals. Those organizations and persons in need are those who ultimately suffer. For example, museums are restricted on exhibitions and purchases, which become entirely missed opportunities to educate the masses. Also, research suffers not because the potentially extraordinary inquiry is unworthy of investigation but due to disbursement restrictions placed by the organization. Furthermore, potential new donors may become discouraged by the boosting of large endowments, while not understanding that their donation is still necessary. Nevertheless, it is up to the trustees to spend the principal or encourage the change in policy.

The philanthropist examined whether perpetual endowments were reasonably desirable and looked at the dangers of a foundation living in perpetuity, five months before the market crash. He approached the discussion with experience as a contributor to charitable causes and also as a trustee of endowed institutions. His insight into the practical side of the problem gives way to the conversation on how best to aid the advancement of public welfare while avoiding living in perpetuity. He provides the example of Andrew Carnegie, who granted to his trustees and successors the authority to change the policy governing the disposition of principal as well as the interest at their discretion. Carnegie believed it was possible to anticipate the needs of future generations.[8] Rosenwald was opposed to any gifts in perpetuity and did not advocate extravagant spending of the principal gift. Instead, he advocated gifts that provided trustees the ability to spend 5 to 10 percent per year, in addition to income that may derive from the donation. Some may make the argument that permission to spend the additional income could lead to decadent spending; however, one must also take into account the temperament of the trustees and their sense of responsibility over the funds entrusted to them. Nor might they understand the responsibility to society that donors and trustees face with finding projects worthy of support—those projects based in education and research that will benefit the masses or specifically the audience of the foundation's mission.

Rosenwald urged that some of the keenest minds become trustees; however, their hands became tied by restrictions of funds available, though the idea behind foundations having a perpetual endowment is to wade through the tide of financial hardship, such as the market crash of 1929. The founder argued that it is those times that unrestricted funds are most important to continue the work until conditions improve, and he believed circumstances always improve. Naturally, as trustees age they become more conservative of funds instead of allocating monies where they would perform at the height of use. Rosenwald proposed radical operation as the antidote, because if funds are expended within a generation, bureaucracy can be avoided. Going back to his highest worry, he questioned the allocation limitations placed on scientific research and education. On a humanitarian note, how will society assist its hopeless and impoverished while the foundation trustees rest with head in hands, observing matters that could be more rapidly improved? Perpetuities, intended or not, demonstrate a lack of confidence in those trusted by the donor to carrying on a legacy. Perhaps the intent behind the organizational design is more of an earthly memorial of the donor than relentlessly efforts to fund discoveries beyond the ordinary, a kind of immortality. Rosenwald noted that the names of Harvard, Yale, Bodley, and Smithson remain a part of the conversation, although not as men but as institutions.[9]

While the concept of sunset is a reflection of the values and norms of the trustees and donors making decisions, it is intentionally shaped by why and how foundation leaders approach the decision and appropriate implementation. As noted in previous chapters, Rosenwald organized the fund with the provision that the endowment should not be treated in perpetuity. The fund may be expended at the discretion of the trustees but must be expended entirely within 25 years of his death. Sunset was an unpopular provision as officials of the Rockefeller Foundation looked down on Embree's judgment to accept a loan with an inflated interest rate when the monetary obligation on said loan was unlikely to be met, while holding onto the fund's large reserve of Sears, Roebuck and Co. stock rather than selling a portion prior to the crash of 1929.

Facing desperate measures and the necessity to preserve Rosenwald's legacy to improve "the well-being for all mankind," Embree scheduled a meeting with Max Mason (1877–1961), president of the General Education Board, administered by the Rockefeller Foundation. Mason appealed to the executive board on the fund's behalf on the common grounds that the General Education Board was also an advocate for the education of blacks in the

South. Mason agreed to grant the fund $200,000 to unpaid beneficiaries, with
the stipulation that each pledge holder was notified of the fund's inability to
meet obligations. Old friend Jackson Davis, General Education Board (GEB)
field agent, would serve as reviewer of all eligible recipients' claims in
person.[10] If appropriate, the organization or individual would be required to
reapply through GEB, where the final decision was tasked to the Rockefeller's executive committee. In essence, those already granted funding had to
reapply but could not be guaranteed award. Those funding requests deemed
worthy remained subject to a second application. Fortunately, the board contributed more than $257,000 to 11 Rosenwald affiliates and 40 African
American primary schools, all of which the fund was obligated to reimburse
Rockefeller. Seventy-one percent was paid within two years of Embree's
initial request, while the balance was forgiven due to the fund and GEB's
overlapping interests in rural schools and vocational shop training for
blacks.[11] This was noted as a contribution toward the board's mission
through collaboration. The significant assistance provided continuity to the
fund's work during the depression, and its stock held in partial perpetuity
accompanied with the market crash would have prematurely ended, leaving
pledge holders without support.

SOCIAL JUSTICE: PHILANTHROPY FOR THE CRITICAL RACE

The word *tzedaka* derives from the Hebrew word *tzedek* (justice). Performing
deeds of justice is perhaps the most important obligation Judaism imposes on
the Jew. From Judaism's perspective, one who gives *tzedaka* is acting justly,
while one who does not give *tzedaka* acts unjustly. Jewish law views this
lack of justice as not only mean-spirited but also illegal. Thus, whenever
Jewish communities were self-governing, Jews were assessed tzedaka just as
everyone today is assessed taxes.[12] In America, no culture held a more unjust
plight than that of African Americans.

Rosenwald, son of Jewish immigrants from Germany, naturally gravitated
toward matters dear to the Jewish and African American communities. It
could be argued that the common history of genocide in both cultures provided Rosenwald a sense of obligation to improve conditions and opportunities that were within his power—not for reasons of notoriety but for matters that would contribute to equality in the present day with long-term benefits. Also, his genuine admiration of and friendship with Booker T. Washington enhanced his yearning to build for the African American community,
calling for specific efforts to increase educational opportunities by financing
the construction and design of more than 5,300 rural schools for African
Americans in the South. Rosenwald did not challenge segregation or the Jim

Julius Rosenwald at Tuskegee University, spring 1922, with a group of young ladies. *Fisk University, John Hope and Aurelia E. Franklin Library, Special Collections, Julius Rosenwald Fund Collection, supplement 2, series 7, photographs, box 24f.*

Crow way of living to change the error of ways; rather, his charitable approach aimed to overturn public policy with social justice philanthropy.

Microaggressions are behaviors and statements that overtly show malicious intent but inflict injury, fueling an unhealthy mental state of the oppressed to a point where they are unable to pull themselves up by their bootstraps, as the bootstraps do not nexistent. In this case, it would not be slavery but rather the false hopes of reconstruction, the actual inequality within *Plessy v. Ferguson* (1896), and the Jim Crow era upheld by local public policies of segregation.[13] To address racial microaggressions toward blacks and the need to rectify them with philanthropy, we briefly examine critical race theory. Initially used in legal studies and civil rights scholarship, critical race theory also draws from literature based on sociology, history, ethnic studies, and women's studies. The theory offers insight and perspectives that may guide our efforts to identify, analyze, and ultimately transform the structural and cultural aspects of literacy that maintain subordinate and dominate racial positions.[14] This theory arrived nearly 80 years after the 1917 creation of the Julius Rosenwald Fund. However, I believe in closing that it is important to highlight how the perceived need of African Americans not only was based in Jewish tradition but also remains theoretically sound with modern-day analysis.

These microaggressions living within public policy had real effects on literacy within the African American culture, including a negative racial climate. The South was a rural place that delayed industrial growth as whites relied heavily on the customs of slavery, later denounced by the Emancipation Proclamation but swiftly exchanged with the Jim Crow era. The region sought to restrict, in various forms, the growth of blacks. In reality, the entire American South suffered. Rosenwald understood the plight of the culture and his cultural duty to help sustain a person before offering a substantial gift in a dignified manner, by extending a suitable loan, or by helping them find employment or establish themselves in business to make it unnecessary for them to become dependent on others. The philanthropist fulfilled his charitable obligation from the heart in the form of social justice philanthropy, which is based on six objectives:

1. Focus on the root causes of economic, racial, and social injustice.
2. Strive to include the people who are affected by those injustices as leaders and decision makers.
3. Aim to make the field of philanthropy more accessible and diverse.
4. Foundations are accountable, transparent, and responsive in their grant making.
5. Donors and foundations act as allies to social justice movements by contributing not only monetary resources but also their time, knowledge, skills, and access.
6. Foundations use their assets and investments, alongside grant-making dollars, to support their social justice missions. [15]

Rosenwald implemented social justice philanthropy through creating counterspaces, which serve as sites where negative notions of blacks could be challenged, inspiring the group's creativity. These effective spaces included the rural school buildings; school, black college, and community libraries; the gift of fellowships and scholarships to promising scholars and visual artists; training of library and medical professionals; and the participation and sponsorship of the Race Relations Department at Fisk University. Arguably, Rosenwald achieved this more than other philanthropy due to his widespread arenas during the early to mid-20th century.

The Julius Rosenwald Fund was beyond monumental and appropriately built to sunset. It was religiously committed to serving a culture that was purposely held back. No, Rosenwald did not challenge segregationists but led by example with social justice philanthropy that would hopefully, in time, right those wrongs that plagued the progression of a culture—actually, the entire American nature. The fund demonstrated that stereotypes and preconceived notions about African American literacy were held without truth. Once given the opportunity and necessary materials, the culture soared. The bootstraps in which African Americans were to "grab a hold of," per se, were created thanks to Julius Rosenwald and the fund. In addition, his relentless efforts and collaborations inspired a number of private and state government agencies to contribute and change policies related to funding stipulations that would benefit the African American culture, a culture disadvantaged by design.

As I always say, you must find your gift to understand your purpose. That gift is solely for you, but your purpose is not. Julius Rosenwald found his purpose in philanthropy for the well-being of mankind.

NOTES

1. Jewish Virtual Library, "Eight Levels of Charitable Giving," accessed June 3, 2019, http://www.jewishvirtuallibrary.org/eight-leels-of-charitable-giving.

2. E. R. Embree, *Julius Rosenwald Fund, 1917–1936* (Chicago: Chicago University Press, 1936), 5.

3. M. B. Katz, *In the Shadow of the Poorhouse*, 10th ed. (New York: Basic Books, 1996), 214–24.

4. Sears Archives, Julius Rosenwald (1862–1932), accessed June 3, 2019, http://www.searsarchives.com.

5. Embree, *Julius Rosenwald Fund, 1917–1936*, 8. See also P. M. Ascoli, *Julius Rosenwald: The Man Who Built Sears, Roebuck and Advanced the Cause of Black Education in the American South* (Bloomington: Indiana University Press, 2006), 383–91.

6. Ascoli, *Julius Rosenwald*, 391.

7. Embree, *Julius Rosenwald Fund, 1917–1936*, 3–4.

8. J. Rosenwald, "Principles of Public Giving," *Atlantic Monthly*, May 1929, 7.

9. Ibid., 9.

10. Ascoli, *Julius Rosenwald*, 392.

11. Ibid., 394.

12. Jewish Virtual Library, "Charity (Tzedakah)," accessed June 3, 2019, http://www.jewishvirtuallibrary.org/what-is-tzedakah.

13. R. Delgado and J. Stefancic, *Critical Race Theory: An Introduction*, 2nd ed. (New York: New York University Press, 2012).

14. D. Solorzano, M. Ceja, and T. Yosso, "Critical Race Theory, Racial Microaggressions, and Campus Racial Culture Climate: The Experiences of African American College Students in Race, Equity, and Affirmative Action in U.S. Higher Education," *Journal of Negro Education* 69, nos. 1/2 (Winter/Spring 2000), 6–73.

15. "Social Justice Philanthropy," Resource Generation, accessed June 3, 2019, https://resourcegeneration.org/what-we-do/social-justice-philanthropy-and-giving.

Index

About the Author

Aisha M. Johnson-Jones is an educator and student of Southern intellectual history, as well as an advocate for untold stories. She is committed to archival research, the production and professional development of archivists and staff, and redefining the scholar.

With a PhD and master's in library and information studies (LIS), Johnson-Jones stands on a soapbox for unveiling the history of underrepresented communities through the use of historical documents. She has focused much of her research on the development of literacy in the African American community and philanthropic efforts to develop public libraries in the South. Her advocacy for archives is conveyed not only in her research but also through her professional career.

She entered the LIS field thirteen years ago and has become experienced in archives management, curriculum development, instruction, and program evaluation. With such a dedication to the field, Johnson-Jones encourages redefining the scholar. As a manager, she promotes her breeding scholars initiative, which introduces high school and college students to archival research and places the focus on synthesis.

Follow her journey of bridging works in LIS and archival studies on Twitter and Instagram @DrArchivist.